Math Expressions

Volume 2

Developed by
The Children's Math Worlds Research Project

PROJECT DIRECTOR AND AUTHOR
Dr. Karen C. Fuson

This material is based upon work supported by the
National Science Foundation
under Grant Numbers
ESI-9816320, REC-9806020, and RED-935373.

Any opinions, findings, and conclusions, or recommendations expressed in this material
are those of the author and do not necessarily reflect the views of the National Science Foundation.

HOUGHTON MIFFLIN HARCOURT

Teacher Reviewers

Kindergarten
Patricia Stroh Sugiyama
Wilmette, Illinois

Barbara Wahle
Evanston, Illinois

Grade 1
Sandra Budson
Newton, Massachusetts

Janet Pecci
Chicago, Illinois

Megan Rees
Chicago, Illinois

Grade 2
Molly Dunn
Danvers, Massachusetts

Agnes Lesnick
Hillside, Illinois

Rita Soto
Chicago, Illinois

Grade 3
Jane Curran
Honesdale, Pennsylvania

Sandra Tucker
Chicago, Illinois

Grade 4
Sara Stoneberg Llibre
Chicago, Illinois

Sheri Roedel
Chicago, Illinois

Grade 5
Todd Atler
Chicago, Illinois

Leah Barry
Norfolk, Massachusetts

Special Thanks
Special thanks to the many teachers, students, parents, principals, writers, researchers, and work-study students who participated in the Children's Math Worlds Research Project over the years.

Credits
Cover art: (t) © Arco Images GmbH/Alamy, (b) Eric Meola/Getty Images
Illustrative art: David Klug
Technical art: Morgan-Cain & Associates

2011 Edition
Copyright © 2009 by Houghton Mifflin Harcourt Publishing Company

ISBN: 978-0-547-47387-1

2 3 4 5 6 7 8 9 10   1421   19 18 17 16 15 14 13 12 11 10

4500237403   X B C D E

VOLUME 2 CONTENTS

* This lesson consists only of activities from the Teacher Edition.

Mini Unit 10 Patterns and Transformations

Unit 11 Ratio, Proportion, and Percent

Mini Unit 12 Three-Dimensional Figures

Big Idea Properties of Three-Dimensional Figures

Extension Lessons

Big Idea Negative Numbers

Glossary

Class Activity

▶ Shifts with Whole Numbers

Jordan earns $243 a week. The money is shown at the right. Answer the questions about how much he will earn over time.

Jordan's Weekly Earnings

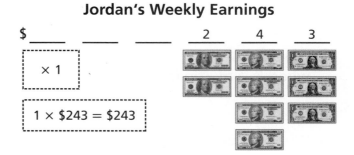

$ ____ ____ ____ 2 4 3

× 1

1 × $243 = $243

1. After 10 weeks, how much will Jordan have earned?

After 10 Weeks

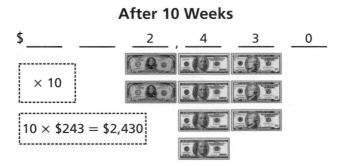

$ ____ ____ 2 , 4 3 0

× 10

10 × $243 = $2,430

2. What happens to each $1-bill when it is multiplied by 10?

3. What happens to each other bill when it is multiplied by 10?

4. When you multiply by 10, does each digit shift to the right or left?

5. How many places does each digit shift?

6. After 100 weeks, how much will Jordan have earned?

After 100 Weeks

$ _____ 2_____ 4_____ , 3_____ 0_____ 0_____

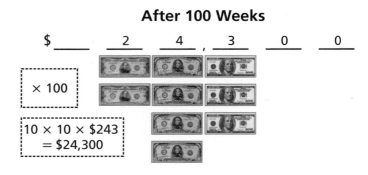

× 100

10 × 10 × $243
= $24,300

7. What happens to each $1-bill when it is multiplied by 100?

8. What happens to each digit when it is multiplied by 100?

9. When you multiply by 100, does each digit shift to the right or left?

10. How many places does each digit shift?

11. After 1,000 weeks, how much will Jordan have earned?

After 1,000 Weeks

$ 2_____ 4_____ 3_____ , 0_____ 0_____ 0_____

× 1000

10 × 10 × 10 × $243 =
$243,000

12. What happens to each $1-bill when it is multiplied by 1,000?

13. What happens to each digit when it is multiplied by 1,000?

14. When you multiply by 1,000, does each digit shift to the right or left?

15. How many places does each digit shift?

Shift Patterns in Multiplication

7-1
Class Activity

▶ See the Shift in Motion

Isabel earns $325 a week. Three students can show how the digits shift at the board when we multiply her earnings.

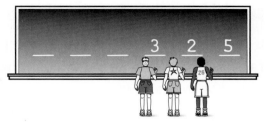

Complete each exercise.

16. Suppose Isabel works for 10 weeks. Find her earnings.

___ ___ ___ $ 3   2   5 |× 10⟩ $___ ___ ___ 3 , 2   5   0

$325 shifts ___ place(s) to the ___. It gets 10 times as great.

17. Suppose Isabel works for 100 weeks. Find her earnings.

___ ___ ___ $ 3   2   5 |× 100⟩ $___ 3   2 , 5   0   0

$325 shifts ___ places to the ___. It gets 100 times as great.

18. Suppose Isabel works for 1,000 weeks. Find her earnings.

___ ___ ___ $ 3   2   5 |× 1,000⟩ $ 3   2   5 , 0   0   0

$325 shifts ___ places to the ___. It gets 1,000 times as great.

Complete each exercise.

19. 567 × 10 = ▮

20. 38 × 1,000 = ▮

21. 912 × 100 = ▮

22. 700 × 10 = ▮

23. The Skyway Express train travels about 800 miles a day. How far does it travel in 10 days?

24. If there are 30 days in April, about how far will the train travel during the month of April?

Class Activity

▶ Shifts with Decimal Amounts

It costs $0.412 (41 and 2/10 cents) for a factory to make a Red Phantom marble. The money is shown here.

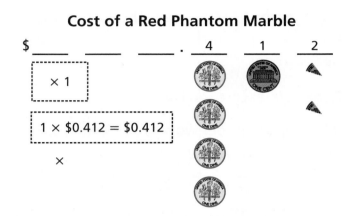

Cost of a Red Phantom Marble

$ ____ ____ ____ . 4 1 2

× 1

1 × $0.412 = $0.412

×

Answer each question about the cost of making different numbers of Red Phantom marbles.

25. How much does it cost to make 10 Red Phantom Marbles?

10 Red Phantom Marbles

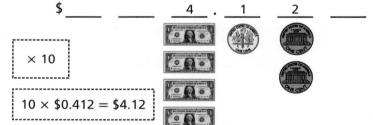

$ ____ ____ 4 . 1 2 ____

× 10

10 × $0.412 = $4.12

26. What happens to each coin when it is multiplied by 10?

27. What happens to each digit?

28. When you multiply by 10, does each digit shift to the right or left?

29. How many places does each digit shift?

Shift Patterns in Multiplication

30. How much does it cost to make 100 Red Phantom Marbles?

100 Red Phantom Marbles

$ ____ 4 1 . 2 0 ____

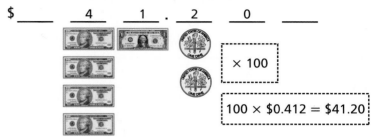

× 100

$100 × \$0.412 = \$41.20$

31. What happens to each coin when you multiply by 100?

32. What happens to each digit?

33. When you multiply by 100, does each digit shift to the right or left?

34. How many places does each digit shift?

35. How much does it cost to make 1,000 Red Phantom Marbles?

1,000 Red Phantom Marbles

$ 4 1 2 . 0 0 ____

× 1,000

$1,000 × \$0.412 = \$412.00$

36. What happens to each coin when you multiply by 1,000?

37. What happens to each digit?

38. When you multiply by 1,000, does each digit shift to the right or left?

39. How many places does each digit shift?

Class Activity

▶ Patterns in Multiplying with Zeros

Discuss patterns you see across each row and down each
column. Then state the Big Idea for multiplying numbers
with zeros.

×	3	30	300	3,000
2	**a.** 2 × 3 = 6	**b.** 2 × 30 = 2 × 3 × 10 = 6 × 10 = 60	**c.** 2 × 300 = 2 × 3 × 100 = 6 × 100 = 600	**d.** 2 × 3,000 = 2 × 3 × 1,000 = 6 × 1,000 = 6,000
20	**e.** 20 × 3 = 2 × 10 × 3 = 6 × 10 = 60	**f.** 20 × 30 = 2 × 10 × 3 × 10 = 6 × 100 = 600	**g.** 20 × 300 = 2 × 10 × 3 × 100 = 6 × 1,000 = 6,000	**h.** 20 × 3,000 = 2 × 10 × 3 × 1,000 = 6 × 10,000 = 60,000
200	**i.** 200 × 3 = 2 × 100 × 3 = 6 × 100 = 600	**j.** 200 × 30 = 2 × 100 × 3 × 10 = 6 × 1,000 = 6,000	**k.** 200 × 300 = 2 × 100 × 3 × 100 = 6 × 10,000 = 60,000	**l.** 200 × 3,000 = 2 × 100 × 3 × 1,000 = 6 × 100,000 = 600,000
2,000	**m.** 2,000 × 3 = 2 × 1,000 × 3 = 6 × 1,000 = 6,000	**n.** 2,000 × 30 = 2 × 1,000 × 3 × 10 = 6 × 10,000 = 60,000	**o.** 2,000 × 300 = 2 × 1,000 × 3 × 100 = 6 × 100,000 = 600,000	**p.** 2,000 × 3,000 = 2 × 1,000 × 3 × 1,000 = 6 × 1,000,000 = 6,000,000

40. Big Idea:

Solve.

41.	42.	43.	44.	45.
60 × 3	60 × 30	600 × 30	600 × 300	6,000 × 30

Dear Family,

Your child worked with multiplication and division problems in Unit 1. Unit 7 of *Math Expressions* guides students as they deepen and extend their mastery of these operations. The main goal of this unit is to enhance skills in multiplying and dividing with whole numbers and decimal numbers. Some additional goals are:

• to solve real-world application problems,

• to use patterns as an aid in calculating,

• to use estimation to check the reasonableness of answers,

• to understand how to convert fractions to decimals,

• to interpret remainders, and

• to analyze and graph real-world data, and summarize with mean, median, and mode.

Your child will learn and practice techniques such as Rectangle Sections, Expanded Notation, and Shift Patterns to gain speed and accuracy in multi-digit and decimal multiplication and division. Money examples will be used in multiplication and division with decimals.

Your child will learn to estimate using rounding and compatible numbers, and then adjust the estimated number. Remainders will be interpreted in real-world contexts, and expressed as fractions or decimals. Students will divide by decimal numbers, and learn to distinguish between multiplication and division when there are decimal numbers.

Throughout Unit 7, your child will solve real-world application problems that require multi-digit multiplication and division. Your child may need more work with the multiplication table, so please support practice with the Target and Multiplication Tables and Division Cards.

If you have any questions, please call or write to me.

Sincerely,
Your child's teacher

Your teacher will give you a copy of this letter.

Estimada familia:

Su niño ya ha estudiado problemas de multiplicación y división en la Unidad 1. La Unidad 7 de *Math Expressions* guía a los estudiantes mientras profundizan y amplían su dominio de estas operaciones. El objetivo principal de la unidad es reforzar las destrezas de multiplicación y división con números enteros y decimales. Algunos objetivos adicionales son:

• resolver problemas con aplicaciones a la vida diaria,

• usar patrones de ayuda para hacer cálculos,

• usar la estimación para comprobar si las respuestas son razonables,

• comprender cómo se convierten las fracciones a decimales,

• interpretar los residuos, y

• analizar y graficar datos de la vida diaria y resumir usando la media, la mediana y la moda.

Su niño aprenderá y practicará técnicas como secciones de rectángulos, notación extendida y patrones de desplazamiento para poder hacer las multiplicaciones y divisiones de números de varios dígitos y decimales con mayor rapidez y exactitud. En las multiplicaciones y divisiones con decimales se usarán ejemplos de dinero.

Su niño aprenderá a estimar usando el redondeo y los números compatibles, y luego a ajustar el número estimado. Los residuos se interpretarán dentro de contextos de la vida diaria y se expresarán como fracciones o decimales. Los estudiantes dividirán por números decimales y aprenderán a distinguir entre la multiplicación y la división con números decimales.

En de la Unidad 7 su niño resolverá problemas con aplicaciones a la vida diaria que requieren multiplicación y división de números de varios dígitos. Tal vez su niño necesite más práctica con la tabla de multiplicar. Por favor apoye a su niño con la práctica de las tablas de multiplicar y las tarjetas de divisiones.

Si tiene alguna duda o comentario, por favor comuníquese conmigo.

Atentamente,
El maestro su niño

Tu maestro te dará una copia de esta carta.

Shift Patterns in Multiplication

Vocabulary

Rectangle Sections
partial products

▶ Solve with Rectangle Sections

Think about finding the area of this rectangle (*Area = length × width*). It would be difficult to find 43 × 67 in one step. But if you broke the rectangle into smaller **Rectangle Sections**, then you could do it.

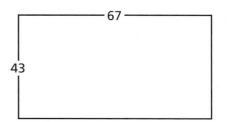

When you multiply larger numbers, you often need to break the problem into smaller parts. The products of these smaller parts are called **partial products**. After you find all the partial products, you can add them together.

1. Explain how Rectangle Sections are used to solve the problem below.

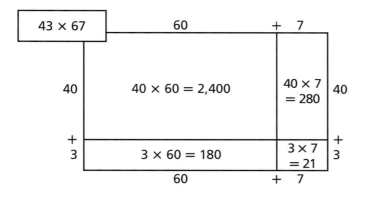

2. Use Rectangle Sections to solve the multiplication problem below.

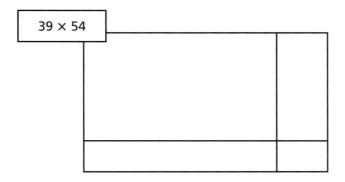

▶ **Solve with Expanded Notation**

Look at the **Expanded Notation** method of solving 43 × 67 below.
Diagrams A and B both show the Expanded Notation method.
Diagram B only shows the results of the steps.

3. How is this method like the Rectangle Sections? How is it
   different?

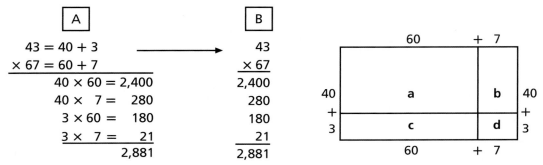

A		B
43 = 40 + 3		43
× 67 = 60 + 7		× 67
40 × 60 = 2,400		2,400
40 × 7 = 280		280
3 × 60 = 180		180
3 × 7 = 21		21
2,881		2,881

4. The rectangle above shows the same problem as Diagrams A and B. Match each
   rectangle section (a, b, c, d) to the 4 partial products shown in the Expanded
   Notation method above.

Solve. Use any method you like.

5. There are 32 cattle cars on today's
   train to Detroit. Each car holds
   28 cows. How many cows are on
   the train?

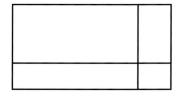

*Show your
work on your paper
or in your journal.*

6. Maria jogs 21 miles every week.
   If there are 52 weeks in a year,
   how many miles does Maria jog
   in a year?

The Area Model for Multiplication

▶ Methods for Two-Digit Multiplication

Look at the multiplication problem shown here. It is solved with another rectangle method called **Rectangle Rows**.

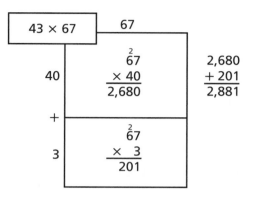

1. Explain the steps of the Rectangle Rows method.

2. How is the Rectangle Rows method alike and different from the Rectangle Sections method you used yesterday?

Show your work on your paper or in your journal.

Use the Rectangle Rows method to solve each problem.

3.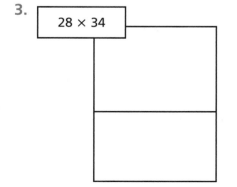

28 × 34

4.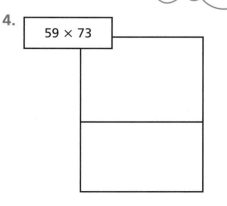

59 × 73

Here, 43 × 67 is solved with a method we call the **Short Cut**.

Step 1	Step 2	Step 3	Step 4	Step 5	Step 6

Step 1	Step 2	Step 3	Step 4	Step 5	Step 6
$\overset{2}{67}$	$\overset{2}{67}$	$\overset{2}{67}$	$\overset{2}{\overset{2}{67}}$	$\overset{2}{\overset{2}{67}}$	$\overset{2}{\overset{2}{67}}$
× 43	× 43	× 43	× 43	× 43	× 43
1	201	201	201	201	201
		0	80	2,680	2,680
					2,881

5. Explain the different steps of this method.

Show your work on your paper or in your journal.

6. Why do we begin Step 3 by putting a zero in the ones place?

7. How is the Short Cut method like the Rectangle Rows method? How is it different?

Multiply Two-Digit Numbers

Class Activity

► Discuss Multiplication Methods

Below are the four multiplication methods your class has tried. Discuss these questions about the methods.

8. How do the 4 partial products in the two top methods relate to the 2 partial products in the two bottom methods?

9. For the Short Cut method, one way starts with the tens and one way starts with the ones. Could we do the other methods by starting with the ones? Explain why or why not.

Rectangle Sections

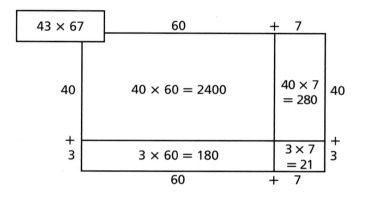

Expanded Notation

$$67 = 60 + 7$$
$$43 = 40 + 3$$
$$40 \times 60 = 2,400$$
$$40 \times 7 = 280$$
$$3 \times 60 = 180$$
$$3 \times 7 = ,21$$
$$2,881$$

Rectangle Rows

43 × 67 | 67

2
67
× 40
2,680

40

2
67
× 3
201

3

2,680
+201
2,881

Short Cut
Multiply by Tens First

2
2
67
× 43
2,680
201
2,881

Short Cut
Multiply by Ones First

2
2
67
× 43
201
2,680
2,881

Solve.

10. 94
   × 36

11. 73
   × 45

12. 69
   × 82

13. 58
   × 70

UNIT 7 LESSON 3

Multiply Two-Digit Numbers **269**

Going Further

▶ Work Backward

Some problems are easiest to solve if you work backward.

Suppose you want to solve this problem: Julian has 5 times as many baseball cards as Carla. Carla has 8 times as many cards as Pete. Pete has 6 cards. How many cards does Julian have?

Answer these questions to solve the problem by working backward.

1. How many cards does Pete have?

2. Carla has 8 times as many cards as Pete. How many cards does Carla have?

3. Julian has 5 times as many cards as Carla. How many cards does Julian have?

4. Look back and check. Write the steps of your check.

Work backward to solve each problem.

5. Barbara spent half of her money at the mall. Then she spent half of what was left at the video store. She had $37 when she came home. How much money did Barbara have when she started at the mall?

6. Paul gave Brenda one third of his pretzels. Brenda shared her pretzels equally with Edwin. Edwin had 40 pretzels. How many pretzels did Paul have before he gave Brenda the pretzels?

7. A number is multiplied by 12 and then that result is doubled. The final result is 288. What is the number?

8. You multiply a number by 10 and then divide the result by 5. The final result is 90. Find the starting number.

Multiply Two-Digit Numbers

▶ Multiply Three-Digit Numbers

1. Below are the four multiplication methods your class has tried. Discuss advantages and disadvantages of each method. Which methods seem better for these problems with larger numbers? Why?

Rectangle Sections

243 × 967	900 +	60 +	7	
200	180,000	12,000	1,400	200
+				+
40	36,000	2,400	280	40
+				+
3	2,700	180	21	3
	900 +	60 +	7	

$$\begin{array}{r} \overset{1\;1\;1\;\;1}{180,000} \\ 12,000 \\ 1,400 \\ 36,000 \\ 2,400 \\ 280 \\ 2,700 \\ 180 \\ 21 \\ \hline 234,981 \end{array}$$

Expanded Notation

$$967 = 900 + 60 + 7$$
$$\times\,243 = 200 + 40 + 3$$

$$\begin{array}{rcl} 200 \times 900 &=& \overset{1\;1\;1\;\;1}{180,000} \\ 200 \times 60 &=& 12,000 \\ 200 \times 7 &=& 1,400 \\ \\ 40 \times 900 &=& 36,000 \\ 40 \times 60 &=& 2,400 \\ 40 \times 7 &=& 280 \\ \\ 3 \times 900 &=& 2,700 \\ 3 \times 60 &=& 180 \\ 3 \times 7 &=& 21 \\ \hline & & 234,981 \end{array}$$

Rectangle Rows

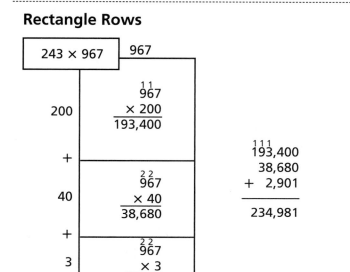

243 × 967	967
200	$\overset{1\;1}{967}$ × 200 = 193,400
+	
40	$\overset{2\;2}{967}$ × 40 = 38,680
+	
3	$\overset{2\;2}{967}$ × 3 = 2,901

$$\begin{array}{r} \overset{1\;1\;1}{193,400} \\ 38,680 \\ +\;\;2,901 \\ \hline 234,981 \end{array}$$

Short Cut

Multiply by Hundreds First		Multiply by Ones First
$\begin{array}{r}\overset{\substack{2\;2\\2\;2\\1\;1}}{967} \\ \times\;\;\;243 \\ \hline \overset{1\;1\;1}{193,400} \\ 38,680 \\ 2,901 \\ \hline 234,981 \end{array}$	**or**	$\begin{array}{r}\overset{\substack{1\;1\\2\;2\\2\;2}}{967} \\ \times\;\;\;243 \\ \hline \overset{1\;1}{2,901} \\ 38,680 \\ 193,400 \\ \hline 234,981 \end{array}$

▶ Word Problems with Large Numbers

Two scientists went to Egypt to measure some of
the ancient monuments there. Help them figure
out the information they need to know.

Solve.

2. The Sphinx is a huge statue with the body of a lion and
   the head of a human. It was built thousands of years ago
   and still sits in the middle of the desert. The Sphinx is
   about 80 yards long. If there are 3 feet in a yard, how
   long is the Sphinx in feet?

3. The base of the Great Pyramid is a square about 150 feet
   on each side. How many square feet of ground does it
   cover?

4. Some of the blocks used to build the pyramids weigh up
   to 14 tons. If a ton is equal to 2,000 pounds, how much
   does one of these large blocks weigh in pounds?

5. If we include the end zones, a football field is 360 feet
   by 160 feet. What is the area of a football field in
   square feet?

6. The largest Egyptian pyramid covers an area as large as
   10 football fields. What area is covered by the largest
   Egyptian pyramid?

7. The scientists stayed in Egypt for a year and traveled
   about 145 miles each day. If there are 365 days in a year,
   how far did they travel that year?

Multiply with Larger Numbers

▶ Patterns with Fives

1. Write an answer to the Puzzled Penguin.

Dear Math Students:

I know that when you multiply two numbers together, the product has the same number of zeros as the two factors. For example, 60 × 20 is 1,200. There are two zeros in the factors (60 and 20) and two zeros in the product (1,200).

I am confused about one thing. I know that 50 × 2 is 100, and I am quite sure that 50 × 4 is 200. In these two problems, there is only one zero in the factors, but there are **two** zeros in the product. The pattern I learned does not seem to be true in these cases.

Did I make a mistake somewhere?

Thank you.
Puzzled Penguin

2. Find each product to complete the chart below. One factor in each problem contains a 5. Discuss the patterns you see for the number of zeros in each product. How does the number of zeros in the product relate to the number of zeros in the factors?

5 × 20	=	5 × 2 × 10	=	10 × 10	=
50 × 40	=	5 × 10 × 4 × 10	=	20 × 100	=
50 × 600	=	5 × 10 × 6 × 100	=	30 × 1,000	=
500 × 800	=	5 × 100 × 8 × 100	=	40 × 10,000	=

3. Find each product to complete the chart below. Again, one factor in each problem contains a 5. How does the number of zeros in the product relate to the number of zeros in the factors?

5×30	=	$5 \times 3 \times 10$	=	15×10	=	▢
50×50	=	$5 \times 10 \times 5 \times 10$	=	25×100	=	▢
50×700	=	$5 \times 10 \times 7 \times 100$	=	$35 \times 1,000$	=	▢
500×900	=	$5 \times 100 \times 9 \times 100$	=	$45 \times 10,000$	=	▢

4. Explain why the product sometimes has an "extra" zero.

▶ Solve Fives-Pattern Problems

Decide how many zeros there will be. Then solve.

5. $\begin{array}{r} 80 \\ \times\ 5 \\ \hline \end{array}$
6. $\begin{array}{r} 70 \\ \times\ 5 \\ \hline \end{array}$
7. $\begin{array}{r} 90 \\ \times\ 50 \\ \hline \end{array}$
8. $\begin{array}{r} 60 \\ \times\ 50 \\ \hline \end{array}$

Solve.

9. Ernesto and his sister Dora are playing a computer game. Ernesto has earned 236 points so far. His sister has earned 50 times as many points. How many points has Dora earned?

10. Mount Whitney is the tallest mountain in the lower 48 states of the United States. It is about 14,500 feet tall. Mount Everest is the tallest mountain in the world. It is twice as tall as Mount Whitney. About how tall is Mount Everest?

Class Activity

▶ Computation Practice

Multiply. Use a separate sheet of paper or work on your MathBoard.

1.   35
   × 90

2.   74
   × 40

3.   67
   × 41

4.   18
   × 72

5.   82
   × 76

6.   96
   × 43

7.   153
   × 79

8.   216
   × 74

9.   653
   × 89

10.   584
    × 75

11.   213
    × 479

12.   406
    × 124

▶ Practice with Word Problems

Solve.

Show your work on your paper or in your journal.

13. The planet Mercury has a diameter of 3,100 miles. Neptune's diameter is 10 times Mercury's diameter. What is Neptune's diameter?

14. A movie theater has 16 rows of seats, with 36 seats in each row. What is the total number of seats in the theater?

15. A large package of toothpicks contains 425 toothpicks. If Kerry buys 24 packages, how many toothpicks will she have?

16. Paolo's car can travel 285 miles on each tank of gasoline. How many miles can the car travel on 20 tanks of gasoline?

17. Farmer Ruben's rectangular wheat field is 789 meters by 854 meters. What is the area of this wheat field?

Going Further

► Estimate Products

Vocabulary

estimate
over-estimate

You can **estimate** to check if an answer is reasonable or to see when an exact answer is not needed. You estimate to find about how many or about how much.

Carrie wants to estimate 411 × 87. She rounds each factor to its greatest place and then multiplies. 411 × 87 is about 36,000.

411 × 87
↓   ↓
400 × 90 = 36,000

Estimate each product.

1. 68 × 41   **2.** 62 × 619   **3.** 57 × 829   **4.** 309 × 513

Sometimes you need to **over-estimate** to be sure you have enough.

Mr. Poy is planning a trip for 64 students. The cost will be $19 per student. To be sure he allows enough money in the budget, he over-estimates. He rounds each factor up and then multiplies. By over-estimating, he knows that $1,400 is more than he needs.

64 × 19
↓   ↓
70 × 20 = 1,400

Solve. Decide whether to estimate, over-estimate, or find the exact answer.

5. There are 21 crates of oranges. Each crate weighs 195 pounds. About how many pounds of oranges are there?

6. Akule's family uses an average of 597 gallons of water per day. About how many gallons will they use in one month?

7. Ms. Long has 12,000 cans of juice. There are 543 students, and there are 18 school days in May. Is there enough for every student to get one can of juice each school day in May? Explain.

8. Erin is making programs for a play. Each program has 9 sheets of paper. Last year, 445 programs were used. Erin wants to over-estimate to be sure she has enough paper. How many sheets of paper should she order?

▶ Decimals in Money Situations

The Ruiz children had a yard sale. They sold some old toys. They made a table to show how many toys they sold and how much money they earned.

jump ropes	9 cents	3 × 9 cents = 27 cents	3 × $0.09 = $0.27
marbles	2 cents	4 × 2 cents = 8 cents	4 × $0.02 = $0.08
toy cars	12 cents	6 × 12 cents = 72 cents	6 × $0.12 = $0.72
puzzles	30 cents	5 × 30 cents = 150 cents	5 × $0.30 = $1.50

1. How did they know the number of decimal places in each product?

2. How much money did they earn?

Mia saves the change from her lunch money each day. She gets $0.34 in change, and she has been saving it for 26 days. Mia used the steps below to find how much money she has saved so far.

$$\$0.34 = \$0.30 + \$0.04$$
$$\underline{\times\ 26 =\quad 20 +\quad 6}$$

Step 1	Multiply by the number in the ones place (6).	6 × $0.04 = 6 × 4 cents = 24 cents = $0.24 6 × $0.30 = 6 × 30 cents = 180 cents = $1.80
Step 2	Multiply by the number in the tens place (2 tens = 20).	20 × $0.04 = 20 × 4 cents = 80 cents = $0.80 20 × $0.30 = 20 × 30 cents = 60 dimes = $6.00
Step 3	Add the partial products.	$8.84

3. How many decimal places are there in the decimal factor (0.34)? How many decimal places are there in the answer?

A bead factory spends $0.346 to make each crystal bead. The steps below show how Antonio finds the total amount the factory spends to make 222 crystal beads.

$$\begin{array}{r} \$0.346 \\ \times \ \ 222 \end{array}$$

Step 1	Multiply by the number in the ones place.	$2 \times \$0.346 =$	$0.692
Step 2	Multiply by the number in the tens place. (2 tens = 20; 0.692 shifts 1 place left.)	$20 \times \$0.346 =$	$6.920
Step 3	Multiply by the number in the hundreds place. (2 hundreds = 200; 0.692 shifts 2 places left.)	$200 \times \$0.346 =$	$69.200
Step 4	Add the partial products.		$76.812

4. How many decimal places are there in the decimal factor (0.346)? How many decimal places are there in the answer?

5. Describe the relationship between the number of decimal places you have seen in a decimal product and the number of decimal places in its decimal factor.

▶ Decimals in Other Situations

6. The owners of the Seven Seas Spice Company want to sell twice as much spice in the future as they do now. The table shows how much spice they sell in a week now and how much they want to sell in the future. Explain how to get the answers by adding.

Cloves	0.3 ton	2 × 0.3 ton = 0.6 ton	because 0.3 + 0.3 = 0.6
Cinnamon	0.004 ton	2 × 0.004 ton = 0.008 ton	because 0.004 + ▨ = ▨
Ginger	0.007 ton	2 × 0.007 ton = 0.014 ton	because ▨ + ▨ = ▨
Pepper	0.6 ton	2 × 0.6 ton = 1.2 tons	because ▨ + ▨ = ▨

7. Look at the number of decimal places in each decimal factor and the number of decimal places in each product. What pattern do you see?

8. Is this the same pattern you saw in problems 1–4?

7-7 Class Activity

▶ Multiply with Decimals

Look at the patterns you have developed in exercises 1–8.

9. State the Big Idea for multiplying a whole number times a decimal number.

Find each product.

10.   0.8
     × 6

11.   0.3
     × 40

12.   0.005
     × 9

13.   0.14
     × 32

14.   0.43
     × 64

Solve.

15. Jesse bought 3 aquariums. Each holds 8.75 gallons of water. How many gallons of water will they hold altogether?

16. Jesse wants to buy 24 angelfish. Each angelfish costs $2.35. What will be the total cost of the angelfish?

17. There are three goldfish in one of Jesse's aquariums. Gus is the smallest. He weighs only 0.98 ounce. Ella weighs 3 times as much as Gus. What is Ella's weight?

18. Otto weighs 7 times as much as Gus. What is Otto's weight?

▶ Zero Patterns in Decimal Places

You have seen patterns in multiplying by multiples of 10. You
have seen patterns in multiplying by decimals. You can use these
two patterns together. The table below shows how you can
multiply decimals by whole numbers, using:
- ones, tens, and hundreds
- tenths, hundredths, and thousandths

x	0.3	0.03	0.003
2	2 × 0.3 = 2 × 3 × 0.1 = 6 × 0.1 = 0.6	2 × 0.03 = 2 × 3 × 0.01 = 6 × 0.01 = 0.06	2 × 0.003 = 2 × 3 × 0.001 = 6 × 0.001 = 0.006
20	20 × 0.3 = 2 × 10 × 3 × 0.1 = 60 × 0.1 = 6.0	20 × 0.03 = 2 × 10 × 3 × 0.01 = 60 × 0.01 = 0.60	20 × 0.003 = 2 × 10 × 3 × 0.001 = 60 × 0.001 = 0.060
200	200 × 0.3 = 2 × 100 × 3 × 0.1 = 600 × 0.1 = 60.0	200 × 0.03 = 2 × 100 × 3 × 0.01 = 600 × 0.01 = 6.00	200 × 0.003 = 2 × 100 × 3 × 0.001 = 600 × 0.001 = 0.600

Find each product using the method shown in the table above.

19. 4 × 0.2 = ▪

20. 5 × 0.6 = ▪

21. 40 × 0.07 = ▪

22. 300 × 0.3 = ▪

23. 200 × 0.08 = ▪

Multiply Decimals with Whole Numbers

Class Activity

▶ Shifts with Decimals

Leon earns $213 a month. The money is shown here. He will save some of it every month.

Leon's Earnings

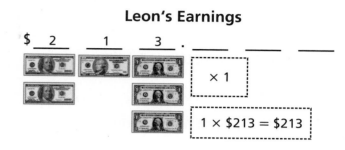

$ __2__ __1__ __3__ . ____ ____ ____

× 1

1 × $213 = $213

Answer the questions about the different savings plans.

1. If he saves 0.1 of his earnings, how much will he save each month?

Save 0.1 Each Month

$ ____ __2__ __1__ . __3__ __0__ ____

× 0.1

0.1 × $213 = $21.30

2. What happens to each bill?

3. What happens to each digit?

4. When you multiply by 0.1, does each digit shift to the right or left?

5. How many places does each digit shift?

6. If he saves 0.01 of his earnings, how much will he save each month?

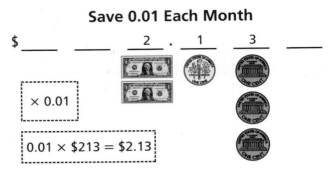

Save 0.01 Each Month

$ ____ \ ____ \ \underset{}{2} \ . \ \underset{}{1} \ \underset{}{3} \ ____$

× 0.01

0.01 × $213 = $2.13

7. What happens to each bill?

8. What happens to each digit?

9. When you multiply by 0.01, does each digit shift to the right or left?

10. How many places does each digit shift?

11. If he saves 0.001 of his earnings, how much will he save each month?

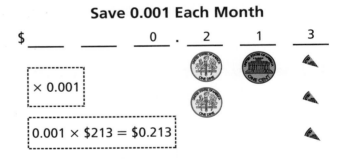

Save 0.001 Each Month

$ ____ \ ____ \ \underset{}{0} \ . \ \underset{}{2} \ \underset{}{1} \ \underset{}{3}$

× 0.001

0.001 × $213 = $0.213

12. What happens to each bill?

13. What happens to each digit?

14. When you multiply by 0.001, does each digit shift to the right or left?

15. How many places does each digit shift?

Multiply by Decimals

Class Activity

▶ See the Shift in Motion

Marla earns $324 a month. She will save some of her money every month. Three students can show how the digits shift at the board.

Complete each exercise.

16. Suppose Marla saves 0.1 of $324 every month.

$ 3 __ 2 __ 4 __ · ___ ___ ___ [× 0.1] ⟩ $__ __ 3 __ 2 __ · 4 __ 0 __ ___

$324 shifts _____ place(s) to the _____. It becomes _____ as much.

17. Suppose Marla saves 0.01 of $324 every month.

$ 3 __ 2 __ 4 __ · ___ ___ ___ [× 0.01] ⟩ $__ __ ___ 3 __ · 2 __ 4 ___

$324 shifts _____ place(s) to the _____. It becomes _____ as much.

18. Suppose Marla saves 0.001 of $324 every month.

$ 3 __ 2 __ 4 __ · ___ ___ ___ [× 0.001] ⟩ $__ ___ 0 __ · 3 __ 2 __ 4

$324 shifts _____ place(s) to the _____. It becomes _____ as much.

Multiply and discuss the pattern.

19. 24 × 0.1 = ▢

    24 × 0.01 = ▢

    24 × 0.001 = ▢

20. 689 × 0.1 = ▢

    689 × 0.01 = ▢

    689 × 0.001 = ▢

21. 42 × 0.01 = ▢

22. 339 × 0.001 = ▢

23. 12 × 0.1 = ▢

24. 59 × 0.01 = ▢

25. 837 × 0.001 = ▢

26. 672 × 0.1 = ▢

▶ Shifts When Both Factors Are Decimals

Multiply by one tenth. Think about what it means to take one tenth of another part. You can think about money.

27. $0.1 \times 0.4 =$ _____ Think: What is one tenth of one tenth? Then, what is one tenth of four tenths?

28. $0.1 \times 0.04 =$ _____ Think: What is one tenth of one hundredth? Then, what is one tenth of four hundredths?

29. How many places did the 4 shift each time you multiplied? _____ In which direction? _____

30. Look at your answers. What pattern do you see in the number of decimal places in the products? How is it related to the number of places in the two factors?

Multiply by one hundredth. Think about what it means to take one hundredth of another part.

31. $0.01 \times 0.4 =$ _____ Think: What is one hundredth of one tenth? Then, what is one hundredth of four tenths?

32. $0.01 \times 0.04 =$ _____ Think: What is one hundredth of one hundredth? Then, what is one hundredth of four hundredths?

33. How many places did the 4 shift each time you multiplied? _____ In which direction? _____

34. Look at your answers. What pattern do you see in the number of decimal places in the products? How is it related to the number of places in the two factors?

35. How could you express the Big Idea about the number of decimal places in the product when you multiply a decimal number by another decimal number? Is it the same as the Big Idea for multiplying a decimal number by a whole number?

36. To multiply by 2 tenths or 2 hundredths, you could think of 2 tenths as 2 × 0.1 and 2 hundredths as 2 × 0.01.

    0.2 × 0.4 = (2 × ▨) × 0.4 = 2 × (0.1 × 0.4) = 2 × 0.04 = ▨

    0.02 × 0.4 = (2 × ▨) × 0.4 = 2 × (0.01 × 0.4) = 2 × 0.004 = ▨

    Is your Big Idea about the number of decimal places in the product still true?

Use the shift pattern to solve each multiplication. Check to see if the Big Idea works.

37. 0.2 × 0.4 = ▨

38. 0.2 × 0.04 = ▨

39. 0.2 × 0.004 = ▨

40. 0.02 × 0.4 = ▨

41. 0.02 × 0.04 = ▨

42. 0.02 × 0.004 = ▨

43. 0.002 × 0.4 = ▨

44. 2 × 0.4 = ▨

Using the Big Idea you just discovered, solve each multiplication.

45. $0.3 \times 0.4 =$ ▮

46. $0.3 \times 0.04 =$ ▮

47. $0.3 \times 0.004 =$ ▮

48. $0.03 \times 0.4 =$ ▮

49. $0.03 \times 0.04 =$ ▮

50. $0.03 \times 0.004 =$ ▮

51. $0.003 \times 0.4 =$ ▮

52. $3 \times 0.4 =$ ▮

Solve.

Show your work on your paper or in your journal.

53. Benjamin bought 6.2 pounds of rice. Each pound cost $0.90. How much did he spend on rice?

54. Sabrina walks 0.85 mile to school. Kirk walks only 0.3 as far as Sabrina. How far does Kirk walk to school?

55. Isabel wrote 4 letters to her pen pals. For each letter she bought a stamp. Each stamp cost $0.60. How much did she spend on stamps?

56. Maura rode her bike 5 laps around the block. Each lap is 0.45 mile. How many miles did she ride?

57. Kim bought 2 pounds of baked turkey that cost $5.98 per pound. What was the total cost?

7-9 Class Activity

▶ Compare Whole Number and Decimal Multipliers

Complete each sentence.

<u>Whole Number Multipliers</u>

1. When you multiply by 10, the number gets _____ times as big. The places shift _____ place(s) to the _____.

3. When you multiply by 100, the number gets _____ times as big. The places shift _____ place(s) to the _____.

5. When you multiply by 1,000, the number gets _____ times as big. The places shift _____ place(s) to the _____.

<u>Decimal Number Multipliers</u>

2. When you multiply by 0.1, the number gets _____ as big. The places shift _____ place(s) to the _____.

4. When you multiply by 0.01, the number gets _____ as big. The places shift _____ place(s) to the _____.

6. When you multiply by 0.001, the number gets _____ as big. The places shift _____ place(s) to the _____.

7. How is multiplying by 10 or 100 or 1,000 like multiplying by 0.1 or 0.01 or 0.001? How is it different?

For each exercise, discuss the shift. Then find each product.

8. $\begin{array}{r} 3.6 \\ \times\ 10 \\ \hline \end{array}$

9. $\begin{array}{r} 3.6 \\ \times\ 0.1 \\ \hline \end{array}$

10. $\begin{array}{r} 3.6 \\ \times\ 100 \\ \hline \end{array}$

11. $\begin{array}{r} 3.6 \\ \times\ 0.01 \\ \hline \end{array}$

12. $\begin{array}{r} 3.6 \\ \times\ 1{,}000 \\ \hline \end{array}$

13. $\begin{array}{r} 3.6 \\ \times\ 0.001 \\ \hline \end{array}$

14. $\begin{array}{r} 3.6 \\ \times\ 1 \\ \hline \end{array}$

15. $\begin{array}{r} 3.6 \\ \times\ 1.0 \\ \hline \end{array}$

▶ Extend and Apply the Big Idea

Zeros at the end of a decimal number do not change the value of the number. Remember this as you explore the Big Idea about the number of decimal places in a product.

These exercises all have an "extra" zero in the product because of the 5-pattern. Complete each multiplication.

16. $0.5 \times 2 = $ ▢

17. $0.08 \times 0.5 = $ ▢

18. $0.06 \times 0.05 = $ ▢

19. $0.4 \times 0.5 = $ ▢

20. Does the Big Idea about the product having the same number of decimal places as the two factors still work?

These problems are all the same, but are expressed in different ways. Multiply.

21. $3 \times 3 = $ ▢

22. $3.0 \times 3 = $ ▢

23. $3.0 \times 3.0 = $ ▢

24. $3.00 \times 3.00 = $ ▢

25. Does the Big Idea about the product having the same number of decimal places as the two factors still work? Do your answers all mean the same thing?

Solve.

26. Ada and her family are canoeing in the wilderness. They carry the canoe along trails between lakes. Their map gives each trail distance in rods. They know that a rod is equal to 5.5 yards. Find each trail distance in yards.

    Show your work on your paper or in your journal.

    Black Bear Trail; 8 rods

    Wild Flower Trail; 9.3 rods

    Dark Cloud Trail; 24.1 rods

27. One of the world's largest diamonds is the Star of Africa, which is 530.2 carats. A carat is about 0.2 gram. What is the weight of the Star of Africa in grams?

Compare Shift Patterns

7–10

Class Activity

▶ Review of Rounding

Round each number.

1. Round 42 to the nearest ten. Which ten is closer to 42?

    50 ⎤
    42
    40 ⎦

2. Round 762 to the nearest hundred. Which hundred is closer to 762?

    800 ⎤
    762
    700 ⎦

3. Round 0.86 to the nearest tenth. Which tenth is closer to 0.86?

    0.9 ⎤
    0.86
    0.8 ⎦

4. Round 0.263 to the nearest hundredth. Which hundredth is closer to 0.263?

    0.27 ⎤
    0.263
    0.26 ⎦

Round to the nearest ten.

5. 46   6. 71   7. 85   8. 928

Round to the nearest hundred.

9. 231   10. 459   11. 893   12. 350

Round to the nearest tenth.

13. 0.73   14. 0.91   15. 0.15   16. 0.483

Round to the nearest hundredth.

17. 0.532   18. 0.609   19. 0.789   20. 0.165

▶ Explore Estimation in Multiplication

For each exercise, round the factors and multiply mentally to find the estimated answer. After finding all the estimated answers, go back and find each exact answer.

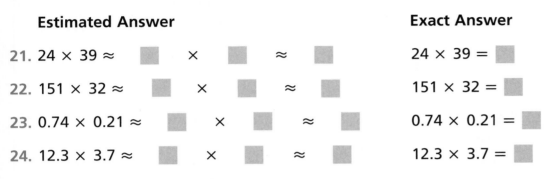

Estimated Answer	Exact Answer
21. $24 \times 39 \approx$ ⬜ $\times$ ⬜ $\approx$ ⬜	$24 \times 39 =$ ⬜
22. $151 \times 32 \approx$ ⬜ $\times$ ⬜ $\approx$ ⬜	$151 \times 32 =$ ⬜
23. $0.74 \times 0.21 \approx$ ⬜ $\times$ ⬜ $\approx$ ⬜	$0.74 \times 0.21 =$ ⬜
24. $12.3 \times 3.7 \approx$ ⬜ $\times$ ⬜ $\approx$ ⬜	$12.3 \times 3.7 =$ ⬜

25. Is there more than one way to round these numbers? Why are some exact answers closer to the estimated answer than others?

▶ Use Estimation to Check Answers

26. Tanya did these multiplications on her calculator.

$24.5 \times 4 = 98$ $0.56 \times 30 = 1.68$ $15.2 \times 2.03 = 30.856$

$0.09 \times 143 = 12.87$ $0.74 \times 12.02 = 88.948$ $9.03 \times 6.9 = 623.07$

How can she use estimation to see if each answer makes sense? Which answers are clearly wrong?

▶ Ordinary Estimations and Safe Estimations

> Dear Math Students:
>
> Yesterday I went to the store to buy 8 bottles of juice for a party. Each bottle cost $2.48 so I rounded to the nearest dollar, which is $2.00. My estimate for the total cost was 8 × $2.00 = $16.00. I had $18.00 in my picket, so I thought everything was fine. When I went to the cashier to pay, I found out that I didn't have enough money. I was very embarrassed.
>
> Is there something wrong with my math? Maybe estimation isn't very helpful when you're buying things. What do you think?
>
> Thank you.
>
> Puzzled Penguin

27. Respond to the Puzzled Penguin in your Math Journal.

For each problem below, decide whether you need to make a safe estimate or an ordinary estimate. Estimate the answer, and then find the exact answer.

Show your work on your paper or in your journal.

28. Michelle and Stacy walked 9.95 miles every day for 14 days. How far did they walk altogether?

Safe estimate or ordinary estimate?

Estimate: ▢   Exact answer: ▢

29. Mrs. Reno is planning to buy 3 bicycles for her children. Each bicycle costs $144.78, including the tax. How much will Mrs. Reno need to buy all 3 bicycles?

Safe estimate or ordinary estimate?

Estimate: ▢   Exact answer: ▢

30. Each bag of soil in the Green Thumb Garden Center weighs 6.89 kilograms. There are 21 bags. What is the total weight of the bags?

Safe estimate or ordinary estimate?

Estimate: ▢   Exact answer: ▢

31. On the Back Explain your answer for problem 29. Which estimation did you choose? Why?

Write your answer to the
"On the Back" question
on your paper or in
your journal.

▶ Practice with Decimals

Suppose you know that 234 × 48 = 11,232. Use this to find each product.

1. 23.4 × 4.8 = ▩

2. 0.234 × 4.8 = ▩

3. 0.234 × 0.48 = ▩

4. 0.48 × 2.34 = ▩

5. 48 × 23.4 = ▩

6. 4.8 × 2.34 = ▩

7. 23.4 × 0.048 = ▩

8. 2.34 × 0.048 = ▩

9. 234 × 4.8 = ▩

10. 48 × 0.234 = ▩

Find each product.

11. 46
   × 0.9

12. 75
   × 0.8

13. 97
   × 0.04

14. 64
   × 0.05

15. 0.346
   × 127

16. 597
   × 0.284

17. 4.59
   × 57.3

18. 0.924
   × 0.865

Round to the nearest tenth.

19. 0.68

20. 0.93

21. 0.841

22. 0.092

Round to the nearest hundredth.

23. 0.492

24. 0.218

25. 0.907

26. 0.569

Class Activity

► Solve Word Problems

Solve.

Show your work on your paper or in your journal.

27. Marcus sails his boat 94.5 miles every day. If he sails for 25 days, how far will he travel in all?

28. The distance around a circle (the circumference) is about 3.14 times the diameter. If a circular table has a diameter of 36 inches, what is the circumference?

29. Nina is reading about red kangaroos. She found out that a male red kangaroo usually weighs about 66 kilograms, and a female red kangaroo usually weighs about 26.5 kilograms. One kilogram is about 2.2 pounds. What is the weight of a male red kangaroo in pounds?

30. What is the weight of a female red kangaroo in pounds?

31. A printer has 395 ink colors and 254 styles of letters (fonts). How many different combinations are possible?

32. Jodie wants to buy a ticket for every basketball game this season. Tickets cost $16.50 each, and there are 15 games this season. How much will Jodie spend on tickets?

Multiplication Practice

Going Further

▶ Use Calculation, Estimation, or Mental Math

There are different ways that you can solve problems depending upon the type of answer that you need.

- If the problem asks for an exact answer then you need to do the calculation.

USE CALCULATION
The cost of a movie ticket is $6.25. If 7 friends go to the movies, how much money will they need?

- If a question uses words such as *about*, *approximately*, *almost*, *nearly*, or *enough*, then you can estimate your answer.

USE ESTIMATION
Hector earns $8.05 per hour. Last week he worked 19.5 hours. About how much did he earn?

- For some problems, you can use mental math.

USE MENTAL MATH
Angela is training for a race. Last week she ran 400 meters 15 times. How many meters did she run altogether?

For each question, write whether to use calculation, estimation, or mental math. Then solve.

1. The Math Club is selling packs of paper for $1.95. The first week they sold 125 packs. The next week they sold 376 packs and the third week they sold 408 packs. About how much money did they collect in all?

2. The Math Club ordered 2,000 packs of paper. Each pack contains 150 sheets of paper. How many sheets is this in all?

3. **On the Back** Write and solve three multiplication word problems. Solve at least one by estimating.

Write your answer to the "On the Back" question on your paper or in your journal.

Multiplication Practice

▶ Compare Division Methods

An airplane travels the same distance every day. It travels 3,822 miles in a week. Compare these methods of dividing that can be used to find how many miles the airplane travels each day.

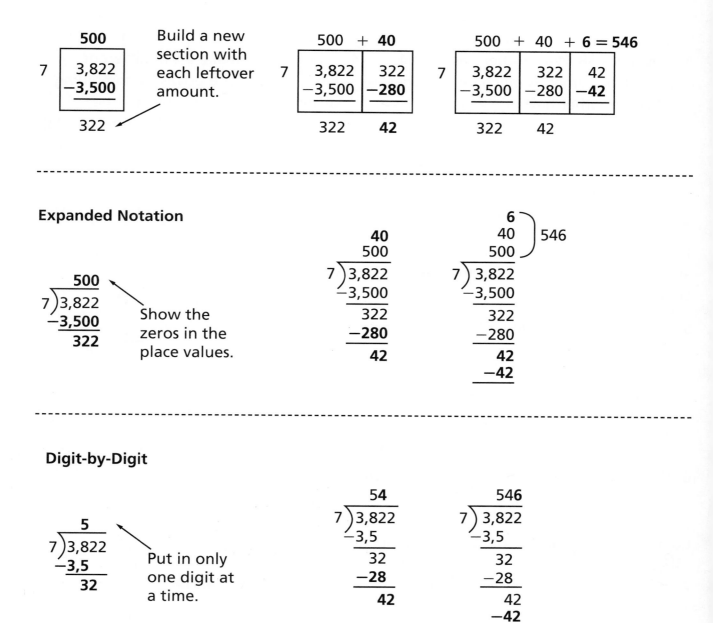

Rectangle Sections

```
     500
    ┌───────┐      Build a new
 7  │ 3,822 │      section with
    │-3,500 │      each leftover
    └───────┘      amount.
     322  ↙
```

```
     500  +  40
    ┌───────┬─────┐
 7  │ 3,822 │ 322 │
    │-3,500 │-280 │
    └───────┴─────┘
     322     42
```

```
     500  +  40  +  6 = 546
    ┌───────┬─────┬────┐
 7  │ 3,822 │ 322 │ 42 │
    │-3,500 │-280 │-42 │
    └───────┴─────┴────┘
     322     42
```

Expanded Notation

```
      500
   7)3,822         Show the
    -3,500         zeros in the
      322          place values.
```

```
       40
      500
   7)3,822
    -3,500
      322
     -280
       42
```

```
        6
       40  )546
      500
   7)3,822
    -3,500
      322
     -280
       42
      -42
```

Digit-by-Digit

```
       5
   7)3,822         Put in only
    -3,5           one digit at
      32           a time.
```

```
      54
   7)3,822
    -3,5
      32
     -28
      42
```

```
     546
   7)3,822
    -3,5
      32
     -28
      42
     -42
```

Vocabulary

remainder

▶ Division Problems

Solve.

1. A farmer has 2,106 cows and 9 barns. If the farmer divides the cows into equal groups, how many cows will he put in each barn?

2. A sidewalk covers 3,372 square feet. If the sidewalk is 4 feet wide, what is its length?

3. Olivia has $8. Her mother has $4,784. How many times as much money does Olivia's mother have as Olivia?

4. A potter can make 2,513 different kinds of pots and bowls by combining different shapes and colors. If he knows how to make 7 different shapes, how many colors does the potter have?

▶ Work with Remainders

This problem might seem unfinished. The leftover number at the bottom is called the **remainder**. We can write the answer like this: 567 R 2

$$
\begin{array}{r}
567 \\
8{\overline{\smash{\big)}\,4{,}538}} \\
-\underline{4\,0} \\
53 \\
-\underline{48} \\
58 \\
-\underline{56} \\
2
\end{array}
$$

5. Could there be a remainder of 9 for the problem? Why or why not?

6. What is the largest possible remainder when dividing by 8?

Complete each division and give the remainder.

7. 6)5,380

8. 7)6,747

9. 5)4,914

Divide Whole Numbers by One Digit

▶ Discuss Estimation Using Compatible Numbers

Miguel has 6 boxes to store 1,350 baseball cards. He divides and finds that each box will have 225 cards. To check, he uses compatible numbers.

$$\begin{array}{r} 225 \\ 6\overline{)1{,}350} \end{array}$$

Use basic divisions for 6: $12 \div 6 = 2$ $18 \div 6 = 3$

$1{,}200 \div 6 = 200$ $1{,}800 \div 6 = 300$

Using compatible numbers, Miguel finds that the quotient should be between 200 and 300. His solution of 225 cards checks.

Solve. Then estimate using compatible numbers to check the solution.

10. $9\overline{)3{,}150}$

11. $3\overline{)2{,}733}$

12. $6\overline{)4{,}560}$

13. $8\overline{)7{,}136}$

14. Kim makes necklaces with colored beads. She has 1,620 beads for 9 necklaces. How many beads does she use for each necklace if they have the same number of beads?

15. The Martinson School bought 1,890 water bottles to distribute to students over a 5-day period. How many bottles are distributed each day?

16. Saul delivers 1,155 newspapers in a 7-day week. How many newspapers does he deliver in a day?

17. Val earns $1,096 a month as a cashier. She makes $8 an hour. How many hours does she work a month?

18. **On the Back** Write and solve two division word problems. Then estimate using compatible numbers to check.

Write your answer to the "On the Back" question on your paper or in your journal.

Divide Whole Numbers by One Digit

▶ Division with Decimal Amounts

Three friends set up a lemonade stand and made $20.25. They will share the money equally. Study the steps below to see how much money each person should get.

When the $20 is split 3 ways, each person gets $6. There is $2 left.	We change the $2 to 20 dimes and add the other 2 dimes. There are 22 dimes.	When we split 22 dimes 3 ways, each person gets 7 dimes. There is 1 dime left.	We change the dime to 10 cents and add the other 5 cents. Now we split 15 cents 3 ways.

$$
\begin{array}{r}
6 \\
3{\overline{)20.25}} \\
-\ 18 \\
\hline
2
\end{array}
\qquad
\begin{array}{r}
6. \\
3{\overline{)20.25}} \\
-\ 18 \\
\hline
2.2
\end{array}
\qquad
\begin{array}{r}
6.7 \\
3{\overline{)20.25}} \\
-\ 18 \\
\hline
2.2 \\
-\ 2.1 \\
\hline
.1
\end{array}
\qquad
\begin{array}{r}
6.75 \\
3{\overline{)20.25}} \\
-\ 18 \\
\hline
2.2 \\
-\ 2.1 \\
\hline
.15 \\
-\ .15
\end{array}
$$

Solve each decimal division exercise.

1. $8{\overline{)47.68}}$ 2. $9{\overline{)58.68}}$ 3. $6{\overline{)316.2}}$

Solve.

4. Imelda has 8.169 meters of rope. She wants to cut it into 3 equal pieces to make jump ropes for her 3 friends. How long will each jump rope be?

Show your work on your paper or in your journal.

5. Tonio has 7.47 pounds of rabbit food. He will divide it equally among his 9 rabbits. How much food will each rabbit get?

6. Discuss how dividing a decimal number is like dividing a whole number.

Use multiplication to help you solve these problems.

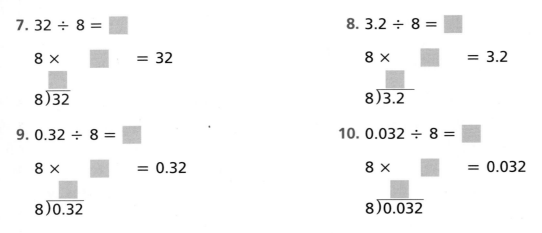

7. $32 \div 8 = $ ▢

   $8 \times$ ▢ $= 32$

   ▢
   $8\overline{)32}$

8. $3.2 \div 8 = $ ▢

   $8 \times$ ▢ $= 3.2$

   ▢
   $8\overline{)3.2}$

9. $0.32 \div 8 = $ ▢

   $8 \times$ ▢ $= 0.32$

   ▢
   $8\overline{)0.32}$

10. $0.032 \div 8 = $ ▢

   $8 \times$ ▢ $= 0.032$

   ▢
   $8\overline{)0.032}$

Solve using mental math. Check using multiplication.

11. $6.3 \div 9 = $ ▢

12. $0.15 \div 3 = $ ▢

13. $4.8 \div 6 = $ ▢

14. $0.021 \div 7 = $ ▢

▶ Add Zeros to the Dividend

Jun must run 6.65 miles every day for practice. She knows that if she runs half of that distance and back again she will have run enough miles. How far should Jun run before she turns around to run back?

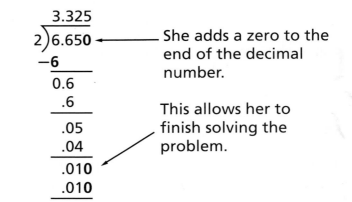

$$\begin{array}{r} 3.325 \\ 2\overline{)6.650} \\ -6 \\ \hline 0.6 \\ .6 \\ \hline .05 \\ .04 \\ \hline .010 \\ .010 \\ \hline \end{array}$$

She adds a zero to the end of the decimal number.

This allows her to finish solving the problem.

15. Discuss whether adding zeros to the end of a decimal number changes its value.

16. Discuss whether adding zeros to whole numbers like 27 changes the value.

17. What is the rule about where you can add zeros without changing the value?

Solve each exercise.

18. $6\overline{)54.75}$

19. $5\overline{)141.2}$

20. $8\overline{)310}$

Class Activity

Show your work on your Activity Workbook page.

▶ Write Fractions as Decimals

Fractions and decimals are both ways to show parts of a whole.

1. Divide 100 pennies into 4 equal parts.   **2.** Divide 100 pennies into 8 equal parts.

3. Write one fourth of a dollar as a decimal number.

4. Write one eighth of a dollar as a decimal number.

Use long division to write each fraction as a decimal.

5. $\frac{1}{4}$ $4\overline{)1.00}$　　**6.** $\frac{2}{4}$ $4\overline{)2.00}$　　**7.** $\frac{3}{4}$ $4\overline{)3.00}$　　**8.** $\frac{1}{8}$ $8\overline{)1.000}$

9. $\frac{2}{8}$ $8\overline{)2.000}$　　**10.** $\frac{3}{8}$ $8\overline{)3.000}$　　**11.** $\frac{4}{8}$ $8\overline{)4.000}$　　**12.** $\frac{5}{8}$ $8\overline{)5.000}$

13. $\frac{6}{8}$ $8\overline{)6.000}$　　**14.** $\frac{7}{8}$ $8\overline{)7.000}$

Use these number lines to discuss questions 15 and 16.

0.00	0.25	0.50	0.75	1.00
$\frac{0}{4}$	$\frac{1}{4}$	$\frac{2}{4}$	$\frac{3}{4}$	$\frac{4}{4}$

0.000	0.125	0.250	0.375	0.500	0.625	0.750	0.875	1.000
$\frac{0}{8}$	$\frac{1}{8}$	$\frac{2}{8}$	$\frac{3}{8}$	$\frac{4}{8}$	$\frac{5}{8}$	$\frac{6}{8}$	$\frac{7}{8}$	$\frac{8}{8}$

15. What patterns do you see?

16. Which decimal numbers are equal in value?

Show your work on your Activity Workbook page.

17. Divide 100 pennies into 5 equal parts.

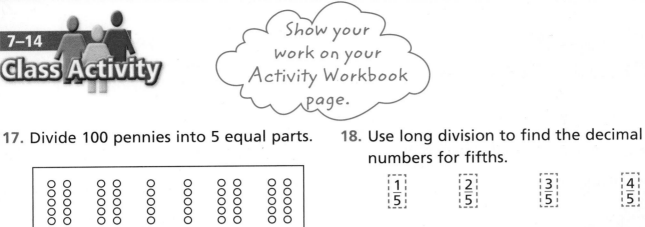

18. Use long division to find the decimal numbers for fifths.

$\frac{1}{5}$ $\frac{2}{5}$ $\frac{3}{5}$ $\frac{4}{5}$

$\overline{)}$ $\overline{)}$ $\overline{)}$ $\overline{)}$

19. Make a number line showing the decimal numbers and fractions for fifths.

0.0   1.0

$\frac{0}{5}$ $\frac{5}{5}$

20. Divide 100 pennies into 3 equal parts.   **21.** Divide 100 pennies into 6 equal parts.

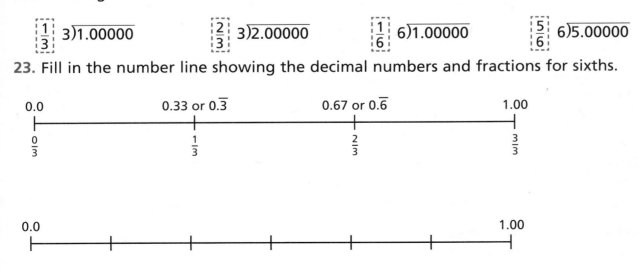

22. Use long division to find the decimal numbers for thirds and sixths.

$\frac{1}{3}$ $3\overline{)1.00000}$ $\frac{2}{3}$ $3\overline{)2.00000}$ $\frac{1}{6}$ $6\overline{)1.00000}$ $\frac{5}{6}$ $6\overline{)5.00000}$

23. Fill in the number line showing the decimal numbers and fractions for sixths.

0.0   0.33 or 0.$\overline{3}$ 0.67 or 0.$\overline{6}$ 1.00

$\frac{0}{3}$ $\frac{1}{3}$ $\frac{2}{3}$ $\frac{3}{3}$

0.0   1.00

Express Fractions as Decimals

► Word Problems

In baseball and softball, a batting average describes how well a player hits. (It is not a mean even though it is called an average!) A player's batting average is a fraction with the number of hits over the number of at bats. These fractions are usually written as decimals with three places.

$\dfrac{3 \text{ hits}}{9 \text{ at bats}}$

Solve. Give the batting average as a fraction and as a decimal.

Show your work on your paper or in your journal.

24. In the first four games of the season, Lauryn got 3 hits in 9 at bats. What was her batting average?

25. Felicia is on a softball team. In her first 8 at bats, she got 5 hits. What was her batting average?

26. On Saturday, Allie played baseball with her family. She had 3 at bats and got 2 hits. What was her batting average?

Solve.

27. Carl's baseball team had a picnic. The coach bought $3\frac{1}{2}$ pounds of potato salad for the picnic, paying $2.25 per pound. How much did the potato salad cost?

28. At the team picnic, the players raced on an obstacle course that the coach planned. The first part of the race was on a trail $\frac{3}{8}$ mile long. The second part was on a park road 0.4 mile long. What was the total length of the race?

Going Further

Vocabulary

divisible
even
odd

▶ Divisibility Rules for 2, 5, and 10

A number is **divisible** by another number if the remainder is zero when the first number is divided by the second number.

45 is divisible by 5 because the remainder is zero.

$$5\overline{)45} \quad 9$$

36 is not divisible by 5 because the remainder is not zero.

$$5\overline{)36} \quad 7\ R1$$

Here are rules you can use to test for divisibility without dividing.

Rule	Example	Example
A number is divisible by 2 if the ones digit is 0, 2, 4, 6, or 8.	136 is divisible by 2.	283 is not divisible by 2.
A number is divisible by 5 if the ones digit is 0 or 5.	1,760 is divisible by 5.	506 is not divisible by 5.
A number is divisible by 10 if the ones digit is 0.	790 is divisible by 10.	809 is not divisible by 10.

Copy and complete the table. Use a check mark to show divisibility.

		24	65	110	108	137	215
1.	divisible by 2						
2.	divisible by 5						
3.	divisible by 10						

Even numbers are divisible by 2. **Odd** numbers are not divisible by 2.

Answer each question.

4. Write 5 numbers between 50 and 100 that are divisible by 5.

5. If a number is divisible by 10, what other numbers is it divisible by? Why?

Express Fractions as Decimals

7-15

Class Activity

Vocabulary

estimate
Digit-by-Digit
Expanded Notation
Rectangle Sections

▶ Experiment with Two-Digit Divisors

When we divide by a two-digit number, we build the unknown factor place by place just as we did before. But now we must **estimate** each number in the answer.

There are 2,048 sheep being sent on a train. Each railroad car holds 32 sheep.

To find how many railroad cars are needed for the sheep, divide 2,048 by 32.

Here are three methods to divide 2,048 by 32. Discuss the steps in each method. Discuss how the methods are alike and different.

Step 1	Step 2	Step 3	Step 4

Digit-by-Digit

Step 1:
$$32\overline{)2,048}$$
(30)
Round the divisor.

Step 2:
$$\begin{array}{r} 6 \\ 32\overline{)2,048} \\ (30) \end{array}$$
Estimate the first digit:
30 goes into 2,000 about 6 times.

Step 3:
$$\begin{array}{r} 6 \\ 32\overline{)2,048} \\ (30)\underline{-1\ 92} \\ 128 \end{array}$$
Multiply and subtract. Bring down 8 ones.

Step 4:
$$\begin{array}{r} 64 \\ 32\overline{)2,048} \\ (30)\underline{-1\ 92} \\ 128 \\ \underline{-128} \end{array}$$
Estimate the next digit and multiply.

Expanded Notation

Step 1:
$$32\overline{)2,048}$$
(30)
Round the divisor.

Step 2:
$$\begin{array}{r} 60 \\ 32\overline{)2,048} \\ (30) \end{array}$$
Estimate the first number:
30 goes into 2,000 about 60 times.

Step 3:
$$\begin{array}{r} 60 \\ 32\overline{)2,048} \\ (30)\underline{-1,920} \\ 128 \end{array}$$
Multiply and subtract.
$60 \times 32 = 1,920$

Step 4:
$$\begin{array}{r} 4\ \\ 60 \\ 32\overline{)2,048} \\ (30)\underline{-1,920} \\ 128 \\ \underline{-128} \end{array} \Big\}64$$
Estimate the next number and multiply.

Rectangle Sections

Step 1:

```
       60
    ┌────────┐
32  │        │
(30)│ 2,048  │
    └────────┘
```
Round the divisor and estimate the first number.

Step 2:

```
       60
    ┌────────┐
32  │ 2,048  │
(30)│ -1,920 │
    └────────┘
       128
```
Multiply and subtract.

Step 3:

```
       60    +
    ┌──────┬─────┐
32  │2,048 │ 128 │
(30)│1,920 │    /│
    └──────┴─────┘
       128
```
Make a new section.

Step 4:

```
       60   +  4
    ┌──────┬──────┐
32  │2,048 │ 128  │
(30)│-1,920│ -128 │
    └──────┴──────┘
       128     0
```
Estimate the next number, and multiply and subtract.

Look at exercises 1–3. Would you round the divisor up or down to estimate the first number? Complete each exercise, using any method you choose.

1. 79)4,032   2. 21)1,533   3. 18)1,061

▶ Does Estimation Always Work?

Complete exercise 4 as a class. Does the rounding give you a correct estimate of the first digit? Does it give you a correct estimate of the next digit? Discuss what you can do to finish the problem.

4. 54)3,509

Complete and discuss each exercise below. Use any method you choose.

5. 74)3,651   6. 42)3,231   7. 23)1,892

▶ Under-Estimating

Here are two ways to divide 5,185 ÷ 85. Discuss each method and answer the questions as a class.

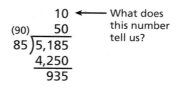

```
         5
(90)
85)5,185
     4 25
       93  ◀——— What does
                 this number
                 tell us?
```

```
        10  ◀——— What does
(90)    50        this number
85)5,185          tell us?
   4,250
     935
```

How do we know that the first estimated number is not right? What number should we try next? Solve the problem using that number.

How do we know that the first estimated number is not right this time? Do we need to erase, or could we just finish solving the problem? Try it.

1. When we estimate with a number that is too big (over-estimate), we have to erase and change the number. When we estimate with a number that is too small (under-estimate), do we always have to erase? Explain your answer.

Show your work on your paper or in your journal.

Solve each division. You may need to adjust one or both of the estimated numbers.

2. 56)4,032

3. 77)4,791

4. 18)798

Think about what kind of divisor is most likely to lead to an estimated number that is wrong. Test your idea by doing the first step of each problem below.

5. $41 \overline{)2,583}$ 6. $34 \overline{)1,525}$ 7. $29 \overline{)928}$ 8. $16 \overline{)1,461}$

9. What kind of divisor is most likely to lead to an estimated number that is wrong? How can you adjust for these cases?

▶ Mixed Practice with Adjusted Estimates

Solve.

10. Hector picked 1,375 oranges in his fruit orchard. He will pack them in crates to take to the market. Each crate holds 24 oranges.

    How many crates will Hector fill?

    How many oranges will be left over?

11. The skateboards at the Speed Demon Shop sell for $76 each. This week the shop owner sold $5,396 worth of skateboards.

    How many skateboards were sold?

12. Ashley's dog Tuffy eats 21 ounces of dog food for each meal. Ashley has 1,620 ounces of food in the house.

    How many meals will Tuffy have before Ashley needs to buy more food?

    How many ounces of food will be left after the last meal?

Class Activity

Show your work on your paper or in your journal.

▶ Decide What to Do with the Remainder

When you divide to solve a problem, you need to decide what to do with the remainder to answer the question.

Think about each of these ways to use a remainder. Solve each problem.

Sometimes you ignore the remainder.

1. The gift-wrapping department of a store has a roll of ribbon 1,780 inches long. It takes 1 yard of ribbon (36 inches) to wrap each gift.

   How many gifts can be wrapped?

   Why do you ignore the remainder?

Sometimes you round up to the next whole number.

2. There are 247 people traveling to the basketball tournament by bus this year. Each bus holds 52 people.

   How many buses will be needed?

   Why do you round up?

Sometimes you use the remainder to form a fraction.

3. The 28 students in Mrs. Colby's class will share 98 slices of pizza equally at the class picnic.

   How many slices will each student get?

   Look at the division shown here. Explain how to get the fraction after you find the remainder.

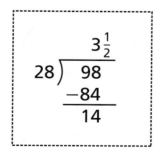

Sometimes you use a decimal number instead of the remainder.

Suppose 16 friends earned $348 at a car wash, and they want to divide the money equally. To find how much each person will get, one of the friends divided as shown here. Each friend will get $21.75.

```
        21.75
  16 ) 348.00
      −32
        28
        16
       120
       112
         80
         80
```

4. A rectangular garden has an area of 882 square meters. The long side of the garden is 35 meters long. How long is the short side?

Sometimes the remainder is the answer to the problem.

5. A bagel shop has 138 bagels to be packed into boxes of 12 to be sold. The extra bagels are for the workers.

   How many bagels will the workers get?
   Why is the remainder the answer?

► **Practice Solving Problems Involving Remainders**

Solve.

Show your work on your paper or in your journal.

6. At the Cactus Flower Cafe, all the tips are divided equally among the waiters. Last night the 16 waiters took in $1,108. How much did each waiter get in tips?

7. A gardener needs to move 2,150 pounds of dirt. He can carry 98 pounds in his wheelbarrow. How many trips will he need to make with the wheelbarrow?

Interpret Remainders

Solve.

> Show your work on your paper or in your journal.

8. Mia must work 133 hours during the month of May. There are 21 working days in May this year. How many hours per day will Mia work if she works the same number of hours each day?

9. Colored markers cost 78 cents each. Pablo has $8.63 in his pocket. How many colored markers can Pablo buy?

10. A meat packer has 180 kilograms of ground meat. He will divide it equally into 50 packages. How much will each package weigh?

11. In volleyball there are 12 players on the court. If 75 people all want to play volleyball at a gym that has more than enough courts, how many of them must sit out at one time?

12. At the Fourth of July celebration, 1,408 ounces of lemonade will be shared equally by 88 people. How many ounces of lemonade will each person get?

13. Armando needs quarters to ride the bus each day. He took $14.87 to the bank and asked to have it changed into quarters. How many quarters did he get?

14. **On the Back** Write and solve two division word problems. Each problem should use a different way to interpret the remainder.

Write your answer to the "On the Back" question on your paper or in your journal.

▶ Use Money to See Shift Patterns

Jordan earns $243 a week. The money is shown here.

Jordan's Earnings in Dollars

$ _____ _____ _____ 2 4 3

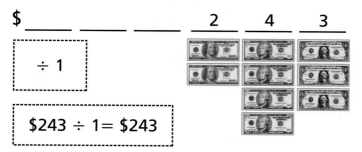

÷ 1

$243 ÷ 1 = $243

Answer each question about how much Jordan earns in coins.

1. How many dimes ($0.10) does he earn?

2. What happens to each dollar? Why?

Jordan's Earnings in Dimes

$ _____ _____ 2 , 4 3 0

1000	100	10
1000	100	10
	100	10
	100	

÷ 0.1

243 ÷ 0.1 = 2,430

3. What happens to the number showing Jordan's earnings? Why?

4. When you divide by 0.1, does each digit shift right or left? Why?

5. How many places does each digit shift? Why?

6. How many pennies ($0.01) does he earn?

7. What happens to each dollar?

8. What happens to the number showing Jordan's earnings?

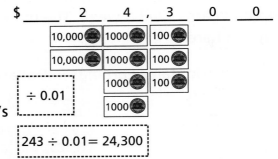

Jordan's Earnings in Pennies

$243 \div 0.01 = 24,300$

9. When you divide by 0.01, does each digit shift right or left? Why?

10. How many places does each digit shift? Why?

11. How many tenths of a cent ($0.001) does he earn?

12. What happens to each dollar?

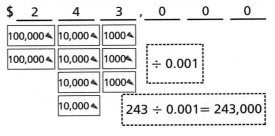

Jordan's Earnings in Tenths of a Cent

$243 \div 0.001 = 243,000$

13. What happens to the number showing Jordan's earnings? Why?

14. When you divide by 0.001, does each digit shift right or left? Why?

15. How many places does each digit shift? Why?

Divide Whole Numbers by Decimal Numbers

► Relate Decimal Division to Multiplication

Solve.

> Show your work on your paper or in your journal.

16. Mrs. Moreno made 1 liter of grape jelly. She will pour it into jars that each hold 0.1 of a liter. How many jars will she need?

    Think: How many tenths are there in 1 whole?

    Complete the equation: $1 \div 0.1 = $ ▨

    This answer is the same as $1 \times$ ▨

17. Mr. Moreno made 2 liters of spaghetti sauce. He will also pour it into jars that each hold 0.1 of a liter. How many jars will he need?

    Think: How many tenths are there in 1 whole?

    In 2 wholes?

    Complete the equation: $2 \div 0.1 = $ ▨

    This answer is the same as $2 \times$ ▨

18. The Morenos made a kiloliter of fruit punch for a large party. They will pour it into punch bowls that each hold 0.01 kiloliter. How many bowls will they need?

    Think: How many hundredths are there in 1 whole?

    Complete the equation: $1 \div 0.01 = $ ▨

    This answer is the same as $1 \times$ ▨

19. Why do we get a larger number when we divide by a decimal number that is less than one?

Dear Math Students:

One of my friends says that dividing a number by one tenth (0.1) is the same as multiplying the number by 10. He also says that dividing by one hundredth (0.01) is the same as multiplying by 100. He thinks this is also true for one thousandth, one millionth, and so on.

Is he right? I don't see how this can be true. Usually multiplication gives us a larger number, and division gives us a smaller number. So this would be very strange. Can you explain it?

Thank you.

Puzzled Penguin

20. Write a response to the Puzzled Penguin.

▶ Change Decimal Divisors to Whole Numbers

It is easier to divide when the divisor is a whole number. We can change the divisor to a whole number by using the strategy below.

Discuss each step used to find 6 ÷ 0.2.

Understand the Division Problem

Step 1: We know that 6 ÷ 0.2 can be written as a fraction: $\longrightarrow$ $6 \div 0.2 = \dfrac{6}{0.2}$

Step 2: We can make an equivalent fraction with a whole number divisor by multiplying the numerator and denominator by 10. Now we can divide 60 by 2. $\longrightarrow$ $\dfrac{6 \times 10}{0.2 \times 10} = \dfrac{60}{2} = 2\overline{)60}$

21. Why will the answer to 60 ÷ 2 be the same as the answer to 6 ÷ 0.2?

7-18 Class Activity

Solve with long division.

Step 1: We can multiply both numbers by 10 in long division format. First, put a decimal point after the whole number.

⟶ $0.2 \overline{)6.}$

Step 2: Then we multiply both numbers by 10, which moves the decimal points one place to the right. We add zeros if necessary:

⟶ $0.2_\wedge \overline{)6.0_\wedge}$

Step 3: We don't have to draw arrows. A little mark called a caret (^) shows where we put the "new" decimal points. Now we divide 60 by 2, just as we did with equivalent fractions.

⟶ $0.2_\wedge \overline{)6.0_\wedge}$ with quotient $30.$

22. Why does moving both decimal points the same number of places give us the same answer?

Answer each question to describe how to find 6 ÷ 0.02 and 6 ÷ 0.002.

23. Suppose you want to find 6 ÷ 0.02.

   By what number can you multiply 0.02 to get a whole number?

   Describe and show how to move the decimal points to solve 6 ÷ 0.02 by long division.

   $0.02 \overline{)6.}$

24. Suppose you want to find 6 ÷ 0.002.

   Describe and show how to move the decimal points to solve 6 ÷ 0.002.

   $0.002 \overline{)6.}$

25. $0.5 \overline{)45}$ 26. $0.07 \overline{)56}$ 27. $0.8 \overline{)496}$ 28. $0.65 \overline{)910}$

➡ 29. **On the Back** Explain why your method for exercise 24 is right.

The cheetah is thinking: "Write your answer to the "On the Back" question on your paper or in your journal."

Divide Whole Numbers by Decimal Numbers

► Use Money to See Shift Patterns

It costs $0.312 (31 cents and $\frac{2}{10}$ cent) to make
one Cat's Eye Marble. The money is shown here.

Cost of a Cat's Eye Marble

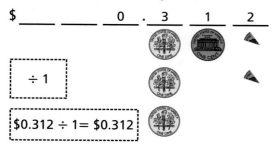

Answer each question about the different coins.

1. How many dimes ($0.10) does it cost to make
   one Cat's Eye Marble? Why?

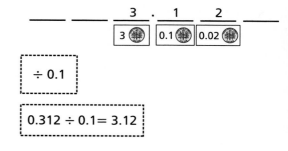

2. What happens to the number that shows
   the cost?

3. When you divide by 0.1 does each digit shift to
   the right or left? Why?

4. How many places does each digit shift? Why?

5. How many cents ($0.01) does it cost to make one Cat's Eye Marble? Why?

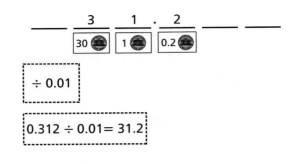

6. What happens to the number that shows the cost?

7. When you divide by 0.01, does each digit shift to the right or left? Why?

8. How many places does each digit shift? Why?

9. How many tenths of a cent ($0.001) does it cost to make one Cat's Eye Marble?

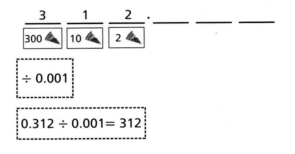

10. What happens to the number that shows the cost?

11. When you divide by 0.001, does each digit shift to the right or left? Why?

12. How many places does each digit shift? Why?

13. Compare the shift pattern in this lesson with the shift pattern in Lesson 18. Is the shift pattern for dividing by decimals the same when the product (dividend) is a decimal number as when the product (dividend) is a whole number? Why or why not?

▶ Change Decimal Divisors to Whole Numbers

What happens when there are two decimal numbers? We can use the same strategy as before, changing the divisor to a whole number.

Discuss each step used to find 0.06 ÷ 0.2.

Understand the Division Problem

Step 1: We know we can write 0.06 ÷ 0.2 as a fraction: ⟶ $0.06 \div 0.2 = \frac{0.06}{0.2}$

Step 2: We can make an equivalent fraction with a whole number divisor by multiplying the numerator and denominator by 10. Now we divide 0.6 by 2. ⟶ $\frac{0.06 \times 10}{0.2 \times 10} = \frac{0.6}{2} = 2\overline{)0.6}$

14. Why does 0.06 ÷ 0.2 give the same answer as 0.6 ÷ 2?

Solve with Long Division

Step 1: We can show this multiplication by 10 in a long division problem. First, we set up the problem: ⟶ $0.2\overline{)\,.06}$

Step 2: Then we multiply both numbers by 10, which moves the decimal points one place to the right. We add zeros if necessary: ⟶ $0.2_{\curvearrowright}\overline{)\,.0_{\curvearrowright}6}$

Step 3: We don't have to draw arrows. The caret (^) shows where each "new" decimal point belongs. Now we divide 0.6 by 2, just as we did with equivalent fractions. ⟶ $0.2_{\wedge}\overline{)\,.0_{\wedge}6}^{\;.3}$

15. Why does moving both decimal points the same number of places give us the same answer?

16. How would you solve 0.06 ÷ 0.02 with long division? What number do you need to multiply by to make 0.02 a whole number?

$$0.02\overline{)0.06}$$

17. How would you solve 0.06 ÷ 0.002 with long division? What number do you need to multiply by to make 0.002 a whole number?

$$0.002\overline{)0.06}$$

Show your work on your paper or in your journal.

Solve each division problem.

18. $0.9\overline{)7.2}$

19. $0.04\overline{)0.364}$

20. $0.6\overline{)0.372}$

21. $0.14\overline{)7.28}$

22. A sand and gravel company has 12.6 tons of gravel to haul today. Each truck can carry 0.9 ton of gravel. How many trucks will be needed?

23. Mountain climbers are climbing a trail that is 3.15 miles long. They can climb about 0.45 mile a day. How many days will it take them to reach the top?

Divide with Two Decimal Numbers

Going Further

▶ Divisibility Rules for 3, 6, and 9

Here are rules you can use to test for divisibility.

Rule	Divisible	Not Divisible
A number is divisible by 3 if the sum of the digits is divisible by 3.	432 is divisible by 3 because $4 + 3 + 2 = 9$ and 9 is divisible by 3.	158 is not divisible by 3 because $1 + 5 + 8 = 14$ and 14 is not divisible by 3.
A number is divisible by 6 if the number is divisible by 2 and 3.	1,242 is divisible by 6 because it is an even number and $1 + 2 + 4 + 2 = 9$ and 9 is divisible by 3.	421 is not divisible by 6 because it is an odd number.
A number is divisible by 9 if the sum of the digits is divisible by 9.	729 is divisible by 9 because $7 + 2 + 9 = 18$ and 18 is divisible by 9.	821 is not divisible by 9 because $8 + 2 + 1 = 11$ and 11 is not divisible by 9.

Copy and complete the table. Use a check mark to show divisibility.

		24	45	54	81	153	427
1.	divisible by 3						
2.	divisible by 6						
3.	divisible by 9						

Answer each question.

4. Write 5 numbers between 50 and 100 that are divisible by 6.

5. If a number is divisible by 9, is it also divisible by 3? Explain.

6. **On the Back** If a number is divisible by 3 or 9, would the number always be divisible by 6? Why?

Write your answer to the "On the Back" question on your paper or in your journal.

Divide with Two Decimal Numbers

► Place Value Concepts in Division

Dear Math Students:

Today I am going to the store with my friend to buy some greeting cards that cost 75 cents each. I have $19.50 to spend. I want to know how many greeting cards I can buy. I solved the problem as shown below, but my friend said it was wrong. He said that if you moved the decimal points two places to the right, then both numbers will get bigger and so your answer will be too big. Is he right? Why or why not?

$$0.75\overline{)19.50} = 0.75\overline{)19.50} = 75\overline{)1,950}$$

Thank you.
Puzzled Penguin

1. Write a response to the Puzzled Penguin.

Suppose you know that 1,715 ÷ 35 = 49. Use this to solve each problem.

2. $35\overline{)17.15}$

3. $35\overline{)171.5}$

4. $0.35\overline{)0.1715}$

5. $35\overline{)17,150}$

6. $3.5\overline{)1,715}$

7. $0.35\overline{)1,715}$

8. $3.5\overline{)17.15}$

9. $0.35\overline{)1.715}$

▶ Check for Reasonable Answers

Solve. Explain how you know your answer is reasonable.

Show your work on your paper or in your journal.

10. The Clark family is having a big lawn party. They have 196 chairs, and they want to put 8 chairs at each table. How many chairs will be left over?

11. Liam needs to buy 640 eggs for a soccer breakfast. If eggs come in cartons of 18, how many cartons should he buy?

12. Jacob made $507 this year delivering newspapers. How much money did he make each month?

13. Ms. Uhura is making 12 skating costumes. She has 21 meters of ribbon. How much ribbon can she use on each costume?

14. A class trip will cost $358.40. There are 28 students in the class. How much will the trip cost per student?

15. The Ramsey family collects and sells maple syrup. Last month they collected 57.8 liters of syrup. They will pour it into bottles that hold 0.85 of a liter. How many bottles will the Ramseys fill?

16. Kyle spent $26.66 on postage stamps today. Each stamp cost 43 cents ($0.43). How many stamps did Kyle buy?

Solve. Check that your answer is reasonable.

17. $0.6\overline{)54}$

18. $0.08\overline{)72}$

19. $0.5\overline{)0.45}$

20. $0.04\overline{)28}$

21. $9\overline{)65}$

22. $0.07\overline{)0.49}$

23. $8\overline{)76}$

24. $0.05\overline{)34.5}$

25. $7\overline{)395}$

26. $0.6\overline{)141}$

27. $33\overline{)3,028}$

28. $0.045\overline{)41.85}$

29. $4\overline{)462}$

30. $0.8\overline{)244}$

31. $42\overline{)4,009}$

32. $0.02\overline{)98.80}$

33. $6\overline{)980}$

34. $0.04\overline{)117}$

35. $19\overline{)392}$

36. $0.081\overline{)64.881}$

37. **On the Back** Write and solve a division problem that uses a whole number and a decimal number.

Write your answer to the "On the Back" question on your paper or in your journal.

Division Practice

▶ Decimal Multiplication or Decimal Division?

For each problem, decide whether you need to multiply or divide. Then solve.

Show your work on your paper or in your journal.

1. A certain turtle can walk 0.2 mile in one hour. How far can the turtle walk in 12 hours? How far can it walk in 0.5 hour?

2. Gus runs 3.6 miles during running practice. He takes a sip of water for every 0.9 mile that he runs. How many sips does Gus take during his running practice?

3. Every year about 135 of the cows on Dixie's Dairy Farm have calves. This year only 0.6 as many cows had calves. How many cows had calves this year?

4. A box of oatmeal holds 1.2 pounds. Each bowl of oatmeal holds 0.08 pound. How many bowls of oatmeal can you get from a box?

5. A rectangular patio has an area of 131.52 square meters. The width of the patio is 9.6 meters. What is its length?

▶ Results of Operations with Whole Numbers and Decimal Numbers

In the equations below, *a* and *b* are whole numbers greater than 1, and *d* is a digit so that 0.*d* is a decimal number less than 1. Answer each question.

6. If $b \times a = c$, is *c* greater or less than *a*? Why?

7. If $0.d \times a = c$, is *c* greater or less than *a*? Why?

8. If $a \div b = c$, is *c* greater or less than *a*? Why?

9. If $a \div 0.d = c$, is *c* greater or less than *a*? Why?

Answer each question without trying to find the value.

10. Which is greater, 42×356 or $356 \div 42$? How do you know?

Distinguish Between Multiplication and Division

11. Which is greater, 0.65 × 561 or 561 ÷ 0.65? How do you know?

12. Which is greater, 832 ÷ 67 or 832 ÷ 0.67? How do you know?

13. Which is greater, 738 × 66 or 738 × 0.66? How do you know?

▶ Make Predictions

Show your work on your paper or in your journal.

Solve.

14. Farmer Ortigoza has 124.6 acres of land. Farmer Ruben has 0.8 times as much land.

   Does Farmer Ruben have more or less than 124.6 acres?

   How many acres does Farmer Ruben have?

15. Mee Young has 48 meters of crepe paper. She will cut it into strips that are each 0.6 meter long.

   Will Mee Young get more or fewer than 48 strips?

   How many strips will Mee Young get?

Solve.

> Show your work on your paper or in your journal.

16. Roberto can lift 115 pounds. His friend Vance can lift 0.9 of that amount.

   Can Vance lift more or less than 115 pounds?

   How many pounds can Vance lift?

17. The Daisy Cafe served 18 liters of hot chocolate today. Each serving was in a cup that held 0.2 liter.

   Did the cafe serve more or fewer than 18 cups of hot chocolate?

   How many cups did the cafe serve?

▶ Mixed Practice

Solve. Check your work.

18. 0.5 × 3 = ▨

19. 0.007 × 6 = ▨

20. 0.4 × 0.8 = ▨

21. 6)5.1

22. 4)22.8

23. 27)8.91

24. 34)1.564

25.   28
  × 0.63

26.   0.35
  ×   94

27.   78.6
  ×   49

28.   215
  × 37

29. 0.8)7.52

30. 0.03)0.285

31. 0.42)15.12

32. 1.9)1.634

Distinguish Between Multiplication and Division

33. 0.37
    × 0.09

34. 0.75
    × 0.14

35. 51.3
    × 6.2

36. 4.29
    × 0.27

37. 0.4$\overline{)0.156}$

38. 0.13$\overline{)689}$

39. 0.57$\overline{)55.86}$

40. 0.96$\overline{)460.8}$

▶ Mixed Real-World Applications

Solve. Check that your answer is reasonable.

Show your work on your paper or in your journal.

41. The Fox Theater has 19 rows of seats with 26 seats in each row. There are 498 people standing in line to see a movie.

    How many people will get in?

    How many people will have to wait until the next movie?

42. Polly bought 12 beach balls for her beach party. She spent $23.64. How much did each beach ball cost?

43. All of the 245 fifth graders at Breezy Point School are going on a trip to the aquarium. Each van can carry 16 students.

    How many vans will be needed for the trip?

44. Today Aaliyah ran 4.5 miles per hour for three fourths (0.75) of an hour.

    How far did Aaliyah run today?

45. **On the Back** Write and solve two word problems involving decimals. One should require multiplication and one should require division.

Write your answer to the "On the Back" question on your paper or in your journal.

Distinguish Between Multiplication and Division

Vocabulary

mean   median
mode   range
outlier

► Leveling Out

Find the **mean** of each set of values. Give an interpretation of the mean.

1. Students collected cans for recycling. Bill had 48, Carla had 16, Brianna and Mario each had 54, and Santo had 53.

2. A waiter quickly poured 5 glasses of water. His boss notices that the water in the glasses are all different levels. The glasses he poured had 8 oz, 6 oz, 5 oz, 11 oz, and 10 oz of water in them.

► Median and Mode

Find the **median** and **mode** for problems 1 and 2 above.

3. Recycling problem: Median = ▢   Mode = ▢

4. Waiter problem: Median = ▢   Mode = ▢

► Range and the Shape of Data

5. Find the **range** for problems 1 and 2.

   Recycling problem: Range = ▢   Waiter problem: Range = ▢

6. Which value or values were **outliers** in the problems above? Explain.

7. How does the existence of **outliers** affect the range of the data? Explain using one of the examples above.

8. Describe the shape of this set of data. Identify outliers, clusters, and gaps.

   26, 24, 29, 22, 35, 29, 23, 37, 35, 36, 24, 52, 35, 25

▶ Whole Number Problems

Solve.

9. The daily high temperatures in Fahrenheit for one week in Minnesota in April were 39°, 41°, 57°, 61°, 64°, 53°, and 37°. To the nearest whole number, what is the mean high temperature for that week?

10. Does the mean describe that week's weather well? Explain.

▶ Decimal Problems

Use what you know about decimals to solve each problem.

11. Gwen measured the temperature in Fahrenheit of a chemical mixture during a science experiment. What was the mean temperature of the mixture? Round to the nearest tenth.

    78.6, 80.2, 88.9, 97.4, 98.6, 96.2, 95.1, 93.8, 90.6, 87.8, 86.2, 80.4

12. Last year, Timothy earned $250 mowing lawns, $128 raking leaves, and $380 shoveling snow. Find Timothy's average earnings per month. Round the average to the nearest cent.

▶ Effects of Changing the Data

Then Timothy remembered that his aunt had paid him $50 for mowing her lawn and $80 for shoveling snow. Copy and complete the table to see how the amount Timothy earned from his aunt affects the data.

13.

	Mowing	Raking	Shoveling	Mean	Median	Mode	Range
Original Data	$250	$128	$380	▨	▨	▨	▨
New Data	▨	$128	▨	▨	▨	▨	▨

▶ The Shape of Data

Any place on earth can be located by latitude and longitude.
Latitude is measured in degrees north or south of the equator.
The amount of daylight—from sunrise to sunset—that a place
gets varies by its latitude. Use the table at the right to complete
the graphs in this activity.

Hours of Daylight by Latitude

Month	30°	40°
January	10:24	9:37
February	11:10	10:42
March	11:57	11:53
April	12:53	13:14
May	14:22	15:22
June	14:04	15:00
July	13:56	14:49
August	13:16	13:48
September	12:23	12:31
October	11:28	11:10
November	10:40	10:01
December	10:14	9:20

14. Draw a graph to show the approximate amount of daylight
    for Philadelphia, PA, for each month. Philadelphia has a
    latitude of 39.95° North.

15. Describe your graph's appearance. In general, what does
    the shape of the graph tell you about how the amount of
    daylight changes throughout the year?

16. The latitude for Jacksonville, FL, is 30.31° North. Make a
    prediction about the shape of its daylight graph compared to
    Philadelphia's graph.

17. Using a second color, draw the graph of daylight hours for
    Jacksonville to check your prediction. Display the data on the
    same graph you used for exercise 14.

18. If you researched similar data for other cities in the world,
    where do you suppose the graph will be almost flat?

19. The North Pole has no daylight in January, February,
    November, and December, and 24 hours of daylight in April
    through August. What will its daylight graph look like?

Going Further

Vocabulary

stem-and-leaf plot

▶ Stem-and-Leaf Plots

Dawn's older sister is on the basketball team at Central College. Her family kept the following list of the team's scores.

98, 91, 55, 86, 74, 80, 75, 97, 85, 70
82, 88, 84, 92, 73, 86, 82, 82, 81, 81

One way to organize and display this data is in a **stem-and-leaf plot**. The results are shown at the right.

Central College Team Points Scored

Stem	Leaf
5	5
6	
7	0 3 4 5
8	0 1 1 2 2 2 4 5 6 6 8
9	1 2 7 8

9 | 2 means 92

1. What does 8 | 5 mean in the stem-and-leaf plot?

2. What is the mode of the data?

3. Does the data show an outlier? Explain.

A rival college's women's basketball team had the scores displayed in this stem-and-leaf plot. Compare the data in the two stem-and-leaf plots.

4. What can you tell about the points scored by the two teams just by looking at the stem-and-leaf plots?

Crosstown College Team Points Scored

Stem	Leaf
4	6 9
5	1 3 4 5 7 8 8
6	0 0 1 1 1
7	2 3 4
8	0 2 3

4 | 9 means 49

5. Compare the median, mode, and range. Explain how you found these measures from the stem-and-leaf plot.

6. Compare the means. Explain how you found them.

Statistics and Graphing

▶ Testing a Hypothesis

Here's your opportunity to design a study to investigate a question of your choice. Your question should lead to a testable hypothesis.

1. Write a question that can be answered by collecting categorical or numerical data using the people or objects in your classroom.

2. What is your hypothesis relating to this topic's question?

3. How will you collect your data? Describe the procedures in detail.

4. Carry out your investigation. Record and organize the data. Make a table to show your data.

5. What kind of graph will be best to display your data?

6. Draw your graph on a separate sheet of paper.

7. Analyze your results. Do the data support your hypothesis? Explain.

8. How could you improve or refine your design?

▶ Polygons on Quilts

Early American patchwork quilts were pieces of material sewn together. Some quilts were pieced together using geometric patterns. Use this crib quilt to answer questions 9 and 10.

9. Draw and name a composite polygon in the quilt that is made up of 3 smaller polygons.

10. Draw and name a composite polygon in the quilt that is made up of 2 smaller polygons.

Many quilters today use "four-square" quilt patterns that are repeated and sewn together to make a quilt.

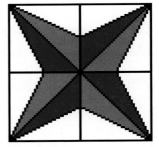

Figure A

11. How many triangles are there in one small square in Figure A?

12. How many of each polygon make up one small square in Figure B?

Figure B

13. Draw pentagons. Show three different ways a pentagon can be a composite figure made up of triangles, quadrilaterals, or both.

Use Mathematical Processes

Multiply. Use mental math when possible.

1. $30 \times 20 =$ ▢

2. $400 \times 70 =$ ▢

3. $50 \times 60 =$ ▢

4. $0.007 \times 10 =$ ▢

5. $3 \times 0.6 =$ ▢

6. $0.4 \times 80 =$ ▢

7. $\begin{array}{r} 47 \\ \times\ 62 \\ \hline \end{array}$

8. $\begin{array}{r} 238 \\ \times\ 65 \\ \hline \end{array}$

9. $\begin{array}{r} 0.62 \\ \times\ 93 \\ \hline \end{array}$

10. $\begin{array}{r} 0.458 \\ \times\ 71 \\ \hline \end{array}$

11. Round to the nearest whole number.   7.52

    Round to the nearest tenth.   0.45

    Round to the nearest hundredth.   0.568

Solve.

12. Paulo's car can travel 38.5 miles on each tank of gasoline. How many miles can it travel on 10 tanks of gasoline?

13. Jessica earns $85 a week. If she works all 52 weeks a year, how much money will she earn in a year?

14. Mr. Solomon's cornfield measures 79.6 meters by 34 meters. What is the area of this field in square meters?

Divide. Check your answer.

15. $7.2 \div 8 =$ ▨

16. $0.63 \div 0.9 =$ ▨

17. $48 \div 0.06 =$ ▨

Solve. Check that your answer is reasonable.

18. $25\overline{)926}$

19. $52\overline{)2,236}$

20. $1.8\overline{)104.4}$

21. $0.29\overline{)986}$

Decide whether to multiply or divide. Then solve the problem.

22. Nadia received these test scores:
    87 83 96 92 82
    What is the mean of her scores?

23. The 16 members of the Shady Oaks softball team had a bake sale to raise money for summer camp. They made $740, and they will share it equally. How much money will each person get?

24. Joseph ran 12.5 miles a day for 25 days. How many miles did he run in all?

25. **Extended Response** Explain why when you divide 64.3 by 0.1, the answer is greater than 64.3.

▶ Exponents and Expressions

A short way to write the expression $6 \times 6 \times 6 \times 6$ is 6^4. You read this as "six to the fourth power." The 6 is the **base** or repeated factor. The 4 is the **exponent**. When you represent a number with a base and an exponent, you are using **exponential form**.

Write in exponential form.

1. three to the tenth power

2. four cubed

3. eight squared

4. $7 \times 7 \times 7 \times 7 \times 7$

5. $4 \times 4 \times 3 \times 3 \times 3 \times 3$

6. $5 \times 5 \times 5 \times 2$

Simplify.

7. $2^3 \times 5$

8. 12^2

9. $10^4 \times 2$

10. $1^3 \times 4^2$

11. $5^2 \times 4$

12. $3^2 \times 2^2$

▶ Exponents and Equations

Solve for n.

13. $3^n = 27$

14. $n^4 = 16$

15. $7^n = 49$

16. $n^3 = 1{,}000$

17. $5^n = 125$

18. $n^5 = 1$

▶ Perfect Squares and Square Roots

Make a drawing to find the square of each number.

19. 8^2

20. 12^2

21. 11^2

Make a drawing to find the square root of each number.

22. $\sqrt{16}$

23. $\sqrt{64}$

24. $\sqrt{81}$

Class Activity

Vocabulary
prime factorization

▶ Explore Factors

Write all the factors of each set of numbers. Circle the common factors.

25. 12, 30

26. 15, 20, 40

▶ Explore Multiples

Write the first six multiples of each set of numbers. Circle the common multiples.

27. 3, 5

28. 4, 8, 12

▶ Prime and Composite Numbers

Write *prime* or *composite* for each number.

29. 29

30. 56

31. 60

32. 99

33. 83

34. 48

▶ Explore Factor Fireworks

Make a factor firework to find the prime factorization of each number.

35. 24

36. 27

37. 30

Dear Family,

In our math class, we are studying algebra, functions, and graphs. Your child will explore exponents, prime factorization, order of operations, and functions to write and solve expressions, equations, and inequalities. Your child will then apply what he or she knows to solving real-world problems that involve one and two operations.

In addition, your child will use the first quadrant of the coordinate plane to graph functions and extend a graph to solve problems. An example is shown below.

Function Table

x	1	2	3	4
y	4	8	12	16

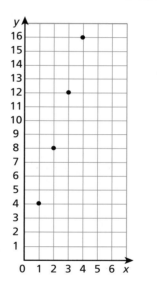

You can be an active part of your child's learning by asking your child to provide answers or examples for the following questions:

- What does 4^3 equal? What does the exponent tell you?

- What is the prime factorization of 12?

- What algebraic expression describes "4 more than 2 times c?"

- What is the function rule for the table shown above?

If you have any questions or comments, please call or write to me.

Sincerely,
Your child's teacher

Your teacher will give you a copy of this letter.

Estimada familia:

En nuestra clase de matemáticas estamos estudiando álgebra, funciones y gráficas. Su hijo/a explorará exponentes, factorización prima, orden de las operaciones y funciones para poder escribir y resolver expresiones, ecuaciones y desigualdades. Su hijo/a luego aplicará lo que ha aprendido para resolver problemas de la vida diaria que incluyan una o dos operaciones.

Además, su hijo/a usará el primer cuadrante del plano de coordenadas para graficar funciones y ampliar una gráfica para resolver problemas. A continuación mostramos un ejemplo.

Tabla de función

x	1	2	3	4
y	4	8	12	16

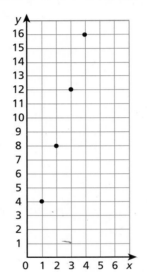

Ud. puede convertirse en parte activa en el proceso de aprendizaje de su hijo/a pidiéndole que dé ejemplos y que responda a las siguientes preguntas:

- ¿Cuánto es 4^3? ¿Qué te indica el exponente?

- ¿Cuál es la factorización prima de 12?

- ¿Qué expresiones algebraicas describen "4 más dos veces c?"

- ¿Cuál es la regla de función para la tabla de arriba?

Si tiene alguna duda o comentario, por favor comuníquese conmigo.

Atentamente,
El maestro de su niño

Tu maestro te dará una copia de esta carta.

Class Activity

Vocabulary

order of operations

▶ Introduce the Order of Operations

$20 - 18 \div 2$ $4 \times (6 + 3)$

Order of Operations
1. Complete operations in Parentheses.
2. Multiply and Divide.
3. Add and Subtract.

You can use a set of rules called the **Order of Operations** to help you find the value of these expressions.

Tell which operation to perform first.

1. $20 - 18 \div 2$ 2. $4 \times (6 + 3)$ 3. $5 + 3 \times 7$

▶ Expressions and Order of Operations

Simplify. Use the order of operations.

4. $25 - (4 + 3) \times 2$ 5. $(12 - 7) \times 5 + 1$ 6. $7 + 3 \times 6$

7. $7 \times (6 + 2)$ 8. $11 - 4 + 6$ 9. $5 \times (12 \div 3) - 5$

▶ Equations and Order of Operations

Solve.

10. $(10 - 6) \div 2 = $ ▨   11. $8 \times (6 \div 3) = $ ▨

12. $16 - (9 \div 3) \times 4 = $ ▨   13. $12 \times 3 \div 6 + 4 = $ ▨

Insert parentheses to make each equation true.

14. $24 \div 8 - 2 = 4$ 15. $8 \times 5 + 6 = 88$ 16. $8 + 16 \div 8 = 3$

17. $7 + 5 \div 2 = 6$ 18. $9 \times 3 - 5 = 22$ 19. $4 + 6 \times 5 = 50$

20. Which equation in exercises 14–19 is true without parentheses?

21. **On the Back** Write and simplify an expression that includes three different operations and parentheses. Show your work and name the operation you perform at each step.

Order of Operations

▶ Solve One-Step Equations

Solve each equation.

1. $k + 3.2 = 8$

   $k = $ ▨

2. $p + 13 = 37$

   $p = $ ▨

3. $40 = 16d$

   $d = $ ▨

4. $77 = w - 30$

   $w = $ ▨

5. $7 \cdot a = 7.07$

   $a = $ ▨

6. $24 = t \div 8$

   $t = $ ▨

7. $3 \times m = 51$

   $m = $ ▨

8. $c \div \frac{1}{2} = 10$

   $c = $ ▨

9. $115 = y + 84$

   $y = $ ▨

Write and solve an equation for problems 10 and 11.

10. David and his friends can hike at an average speed of 5 miles per hour. Write an equation that can be used to estimate the time (t) it will take them to cover 28.3 miles.

11. Kiko has saved \$175. She needs \$450 to get a new bike. Write an equation that can be used to find how much more money she needs to save (m).

12. Write a problem that could be solved using this equation.

    $80 - s = 65$

▶ Parentheses in Equations

Solve. Remember to use the order of operations.

13. $(10 - 4) \cdot 7 = n \cdot 7$

    $n = \boxed{}$

14. $7 \cdot (9 - 3) = t$

    $t = \boxed{}$

15. $(20 - 6) \div 2 = b$

    $b = \boxed{}$

16. $(15 - 7) - (32 \div 8) = \boxed{}$

17. $(17 + 10) \div (7 - 4) = \boxed{}$

18. $(42 \div 7) \cdot (23 - 18) = \boxed{}$

19. $(13 + 27) \div (4 \cdot 2) = \boxed{}$

▶ Solve Two-Step Equations

Use two steps to solve each equation.

20. $8 \div (y + 7) = 1$

    $y = \boxed{}$

21. $3f - 1 = 8$

    $f = \boxed{}$

22. $(g \div 5) + 1 = 2$

    $g = \boxed{}$

23. $2m + 1 = 13$

    $m = \boxed{}$

24. $(d \div 2) + 6 = 7$

    $d = \boxed{}$

25. $4h - 5 = 19$

    $h = \boxed{}$

Write and solve an equation for each problem.

26. It costs $25 plus $10 per hour to rent a canoe. Emilio spent $70 one Saturday to go canoeing. How many hours (h) was he out in the canoe?

27. Janelle is knitting a sweater at the rate of 4 rows per hour. She worked 6 hours yesterday, but that included 1 hour for lunch. How many knitting rows did she finish yesterday?

Class Activity

► Situation Equations

28. Pico is mixing fertilizer in water to feed his plants. cups of water. He puts *x* ounces of fertilizer into ea~~c~~ 3 using 4.5 ounces of fertilizer in all. Write a situation to match this situation.

29. Pico realized that he did not have enough fertilizer mixt for all of his plants. He doubled the number of cups and doubled the total amount of fertilizer he used in all. Writ~ situation equation to match this situation.

30. How are your two situation equations similar?

31. Is the solution equation the same for each situation? How do you know?

► Equality

Use what you know about equality to find the value of the variable.

32. $25 + 8 = h + 25$

$h = $ ▨

33. $a \bullet 6.5 = 6.5 \bullet 20$

$a = $ ▨

34. $\frac{4}{5} \times 10 = m \times \frac{4}{5}$

$m = $ ▨

35. $3.6 + 0.9 = p + 3.6$

$p = $ ▨

36. $(6 \bullet 8) \bullet \frac{3}{4} = 6 \bullet (y \bullet \frac{3}{4})$

$y = $ ▨

37. $k \bullet 67 = 67 \bullet 213$

$k = $ ▨

38. $8 \bullet (15 + w) = (8 \bullet 15) + (8 \bullet 9)$

$w = $ ▨

39. $(d \bullet 16) + (d \bullet 12) = 7 \bullet (16 + 12)$

$d = $ ▨

olution Equations

► Mixed Situation a ___

Write a situation equat ___ d a solution equation using a
variable to represent ___ nown. Solve your equations.

40. Melinda needs ___ sale. of fabric to make a squirrel costume.
She found 3 ___ sale. How much more fabric does she
need to b ___

Situatio ___

Sol ___ itical jars with 10 pints of home-made
___ n. Each jar held 1.25 pints. Then he made a
41. ___ filling the same number of jars. How many jars
___ he fill?

Equation: ___

Equation: ___

___ ater has 15 seats in each row. When all the tickets are
___ , the theater holds 375 people. How many rows of seats
___ there?

___ ituation Equation: ___

Solution Equation: ___

.3. There were some bags of used clothing left after the yard
sale was over. Hal and Patty took 12 bags to a thrift store
and left 3 bags in the basement. How many bags of clothing
were not sold at the yard sale?

Situation Equation: ___

Solution Equation: ___

44. Cesar started with $80 and in 6 weeks had $350. He saved the
same amount per week. How much did he save each week?

Situation Equation: ___

Show the steps in your solution: ___

▶ Substitute a Value

Vocabulary

variable   equation
expression   evaluate

$$3 + d = 12$$

A **variable** is any letter, such as x or d, that you use to stand for a number. $3 + d$ is called an **expression** and $3 + d = 12$ is called an **equation**. Sometimes you solve the equation by finding the value of the variable. Other times, you **evaluate** an expression by substituting a number for the variable.

Substitute the given value for the variable to evaluate each expression.

1. $(80 \div g) - 5$ for $g = 10$

2. $b \bullet (3.2 \div 0.8)$ for $b = 6$

3. $(4 \times \frac{1}{2}) \bullet (7 - w)$ for $w = 3$

4. $(p + 30) \div (98 \div 14)$ for $p = 5$

Evaluate each equation.

5. Is $18 + n = 37$ true for $n = 19$?

6. Is $0.68 = 3.4k$ true for $k = 20$?

7. Is $75 - y \div 5 = 9$ true for $y = 30$?

8. Is $\frac{1}{3} \bullet 57 - a = 10$ true for $a = 9$?

▶ Represent Situations with Expressions

Choose the expression that represents each situation.

9. Elena has a part-time job that pays $10 per hour. Which expression shows how much money she will earn next week if h stands for the number of hours she works?

   a. $\$10 \bullet 7h$ b. $\$10 \bullet h$ c. $\$10 + 7h$

10. Greg started a computer club with 9 of his friends. He hopes to get 5 more people to join each month. Which expression shows the future club membership? The variable m stands for the number of months.

    a. $9 + 5m$ b. $m \bullet (9 + 5)$ c. $10 + 5m$

Vocabulary

inequality

You can find variables in an **inequality** also, such as $d > 5$, $d < 10$, or $d \neq 5$.

▶ Evaluate Inequalities

Choose the values of the variable that make each inequality true.

11. $\frac{1}{4} \bullet t < 30$

    a. $t = 60$ b. $t = 90$ c. $t = 120$ d. $t = 150$

12. $12 - g > 4.5$

    a. $g = 6.5$ b. $g = 7.5$ c. $g = 8.5$ d. $g = 9.5$

13. $60 \leq d - 13$

    a. $d = 47$ b. $d = 50$ c. $d = 73$ d. $d = 90$

▶ Inequality Situations

Choose the inequality that represents each situation.

14. Julie's exercise goal is to walk more than 10 miles each week. Which inequality shows the number of miles (m) she wants to walk next week?

    a. $m > 10$ b. $m < 10$ c. $m \leq 10$

15. Mr. Okano announced that no more than 250 students can go on the spring field trip. Which inequality shows the number of students (s) who can go on the trip?

    a. $s \geq 250$ b. $s \neq 250$ c. $s \leq 250$

16. Write a real-world situation to represent the inequality $k < 150$.

17. Write a real-world situation to represent the inequality $f \geq 4\frac{1}{2}$.

     Evaluate Expressions, Equations, and Inequalities

Class Activity

Show your work on your Activity Workbook page.

▶ Complete a Function Table

Use the given rule to complete each **function** table.

1.

Rule in Words	Multiply by 4, then subtract 2.					
Input	1	2	3	■	■	■
Output	■	■	■	14	18	22

2.

Rule in Words	Multiply by 20, then add 5.					
Input	1	2	■	■	5	6
Output	■	■	65	85	■	■

3.

Rule in Words	Divide by 5, then add 1.					
Input	10	20	■	40	■	60
Output	■	■	7	■	11	■

▶ Rules for Functions

Complete the rule for each function table.

4.

Rule in Words	Divide by 2, then add _____.				
Input	2	4	6	8	10
Output	11	12	13	14	15

5.

Rule in Words	Multiply by _____, then subtract 2.				
Input	1	2	3	4	5
Output	3	8	13	18	23

Show your work on your Activity Workbook page.

▶ Functions and Equations

Use the equation to complete each function table.

6.

Equation	$y = 3x + 8$				
Input (x)	0	1	2	3	4
Output (y)	8	▣	▣	▣	▣

7.

Equation	$y = (x \div 10) + 3$				
Input (x)	20	30	40	50	60
Output (y)	5	▣	▣	▣	▣

8.

Equation	$y = 10x - 1$				
Input (x)	1	2	3	4	5
Output (y)	9	▣	▣	▣	▣

For each function table, complete the rule, and then write an equation.

9.

Rule in Words	Multiply by 2, then add _____ ▣.				
Equation	▣				
Input (x)	1	2	3	4	5
Output (y)	9	11	13	15	17

10.

Rule in Words	Divide by _____ ▣, then subtract 4.				
Equation	▣				
Input (x)	12	24	36	48	60
Output (y)	0	4	8	12	16

Functions and Equations

Class Activity

▶ Equations for Real-World Situations

Write the equation for each function table.

11. George has plans to save $15 each week. The table shows his total savings (*s*) for any number of weeks (*w*).

Number of weeks (*w*)	1	2	3	4	5
Total savings (*s*)	$15	$30	$45	$60	$75

Using the variables *s* and *w*, write an equation that shows the savings (*s*) is a function of the number of weeks (*w*).

12. A group of bird watchers hikes 8 miles in the morning, then 2 miles for each hour in the afternoon. The table shows the total miles (*m*) hiked for any number of afternoon hiking hours (*h*).

Afternoon hours (*h*)	1	2	3	4	5
Total miles hiked (*m*)	10	12	14	16	18

Using the variables *m* and *h*, write an equation that shows the total miles (*m*) is a function of the number of hours of afternoon hiking (*h*).

13. The square dance club had 400 members, but has been losing about 10 members each month. The table estimates the membership (*m*) after any number of months (*n*).

Number of months (*n*)	6	12	18	24	30
Membership (*m*)	340	280	220	160	100

Using the variables *m* and *n*, write an equation that shows the membership (*m*) is a function of the number of months (*n*).

Show your work on your Activity Workbook page.

▶ Solve Problems Using Function Tables

Complete the function table to solve each problem.

14. Hank is reading a book about a famous scientist. He plans to read 12 pages each day.

Number of days (n)	1	2	3	4	5
Total pages read (p)	12				

How many pages will Hank have read in 5 days?

15. Each family going to the school play must make a $10 donation. In addition, the play tickets cost $2 each.

Number of tickets (t)	2	3	4	5	6
Cost in dollars (d)	$14				

Xavier's family buys 6 tickets. What is the total cost?

16. Johanna has $120 for spending money on her trip. She estimates she will spend $20 per day.

Number of days (n)	1	2	3	4	5
Money remaining (d)	$100				

How much does Johanna have left after 3 days?

17. Sal and Yoko have a leaf-raking business. For each house, they charge $3.50 per hour plus an additional $10 to haul away the leaves in bags.

Number of hours (h)	2	3	4	5	6
Money earned (e)	$17				

It takes them 5 hours to rake the leaves at Uncle Bob's house. How much do they make?

Functions and Equations

Class Activity

Show your work on your Activity Workbook page.

Vocabulary

coordinate plane
x-axis
y-axis
ordered pair

▶ Plot and Locate Points

A **coordinate plane** is a grid that has a horizontal axis (*x*-axis) and a vertical axis (*y*-axis). We can name any point on the grid using an **ordered pair** (*x, y*) where *x* and *y* are the coordinates that represent distance.

The *x*-coordinate is first. It tells the horizontal distance from 0 along the *x*-axis. The *y*-coordinate is second. It tells the vertical distance from the *x*-axis along the *y*-axis.

On this grid, the location of point *A* is (2, 1): 2 units to the right of 0 and 1 unit up from 0.

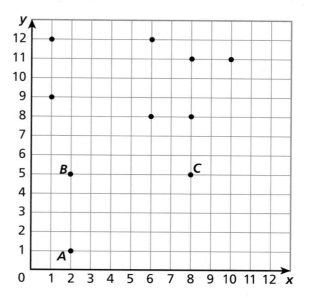

Write the missing coordinates.

1. *B* is (2, _____).

2. *C* is (_____, _____).

3. Using your ruler, draw a line segment from point *A* to point *B* and from point *B* to point *C*. These line segments form two sides of a rectangle.

4. What is the location of the point *D* that completes the rectangle? (_____, _____)

5. Draw point *D* and label it. Draw two line segments to complete the rectangle. These are line segments _____ and _____.

Find these points and connect them. Then name the new figures.

6. *E* is (1, 9). *F* is (1, 12). *G* is (6, 12). *EFG* is a _____.

7. *H* is (6, 8). *I* is (8, 11). *J* is (10, 11). *K* is (8, 8).
   HIJK is a _____.

▶ Horizontal and Vertical Distance

8. On the grid below, plot a point at (4, 2) and label the point *A*, plot a
   point at (11, 2) and label the point *I*, plot a point at (11, 12) and label
   the point *E*, and plot a point at (4, 12) and label the point *U*. Then use
   a ruler and connect the points to form a quadrilateral.

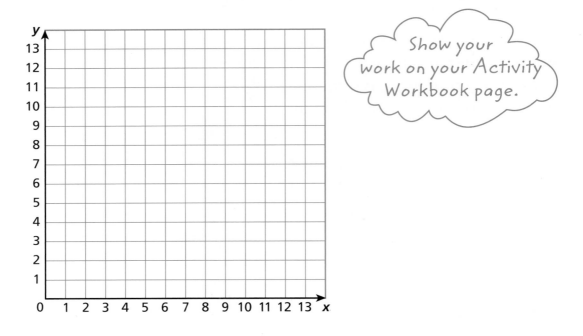

Show your work on your Activity Workbook page.

9. Explain how subtraction can be used to find the lengths
   of $\overline{AI}$ and $\overline{IE}$. Then use subtraction to find the lengths.

10. Write an equation to represent the perimeter of *ABCD*.

11. On the grid above, draw a rectangle that is not a square. What
    ordered pairs represent the vertices of your rectangle?

12. What is the perimeter of your rectangle? Explain your answer.

Going Further

▶ Find Routes

This is a grid map of the streets in the community where Abdi lives.

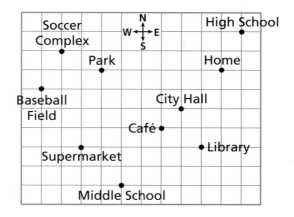

Solve.

1. Describe the shortest route from Abdi's home to the supermarket. Include the words *north, south, east, west, left,* and/or *right* in your answer, whenever possible.

2. What is the shortest route from the park to Abdi's home if stops must be made at the high school and at the library? Write your answer as a number of blocks.

3. How many different paths from the middle school to the café are exactly five blocks long?

Going Further

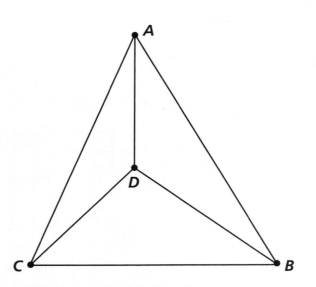

▶ Points and Paths

The distances between points
A, B, C, and D are shown below.

A to B = 20 miles
A to C = 18 miles
A to D = 9 miles
B to C = 16 miles
B to D = 12 miles
C to D = 10 miles

4. Find the shortest path, beginning and ending at point *A*, which
passes through points *B*, *C*, and *D* in any order.

a. What is the length of that path?

b. Describe the path.

*Show your
work on your Activity
Workbook page.*

Draw a path that connects <u>all</u> of the points. You cannot lift your pencil,
cross over a path or retrace any portion of any path.

5.

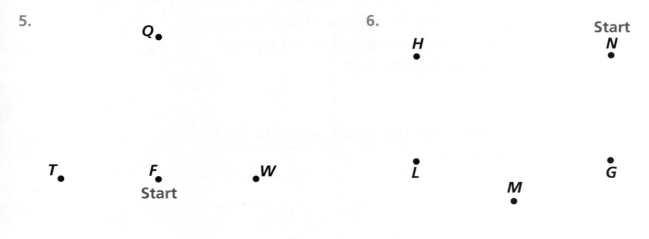

6.

Coordinate Graphs in the First Quadrant

Show your work on your Activity Workbook page.

▶ Graph a Function

A **function** can be described by an equation, by a table that shows ordered pairs of numbers, by a verbal rule, or by a line on a coordinate graph made by connecting ordered pairs.

1. Mindy and her friends are planning to walk for a charity. They will earn the same number of dollars (*d*) for each mile (*m*) they walk. Fill in the 4 tables to show what they could earn for charity.

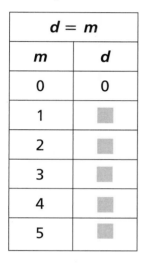

$d = m$	
m	**d**
0	0
1	▨
2	▨
3	▨
4	▨
5	▨

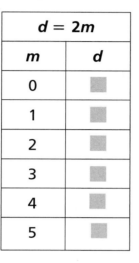

$d = 2m$	
m	**d**
0	▨
1	▨
2	▨
3	▨
4	▨
5	▨

$d = 3m$	
m	**d**
0	▨
1	▨
2	▨
3	▨
4	▨
5	▨

$d = 5m$	
m	**d**
0	▨
1	▨
2	▨
3	▨
4	▨
5	▨

2. For each table, graph the ordered pairs and connect the points with a line (use your ruler to draw the line). Label each line with its equation.

3. Give 2 coordinate pairs you could use to graph $d = 4m$.

   (___▨___, ___▨___) and (___▨___, ___▨___)

Draw and label this line.

4. Describe relationships you see.

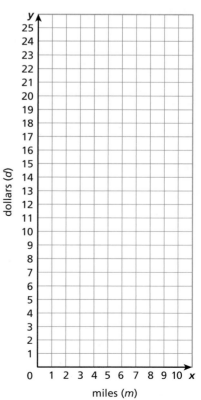

Class Activity

Show your work on your Activity Workbook page.

▶ Use a Verbal Rule to Graph a Function

Functions can also describe additive relations. In these tables, *s* is age of a sister and *b* is the age of a brother. Discuss what each table tells you about their ages.

s = b	
b	s
0	
1	
2	
3	
4	
5	

s = b + 1	
b	s
0	
1	
2	
3	
4	
5	

s = b + 2	
b	s
0	
1	
2	
3	
4	
5	

s = b + 3	
b	s
0	
1	
2	
3	
4	
5	

s = b + 4	
b	s
0	
1	
2	
3	
4	
5	

5. For each table, graph the ordered pairs and connect the points with a line (use your ruler to draw the line). Label each line with its equation.

6. Give 2 coordinate pairs you could use to graph $s = b + 10$.

(_____, _____) and (_____, _____)

Draw and label this line.

7. Describe relationships you see.

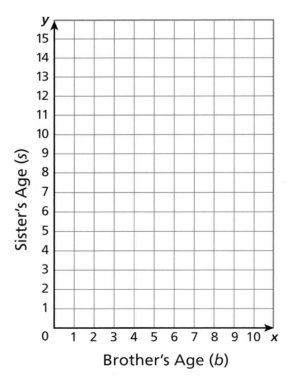

Sister's Age (s)

Brother's Age (b)

Show your work on your Activity Workbook page.

▶ Patterns in Function Lines

Functions are often given using *x* and *y*.

8. Complete each function table.

9. Write the rule in words for each equation.

y = x

y = 2x

y = x + 2

y = x		y = 2x		y = x + 2	
x	y	x	y	x	y
0		0		0	
1		1		1	
2		2		2	
3		3		3	
4		4		4	
5		5		5	

10. Plot the coordinates from each table. Draw a line to connect each set of points. Label each line with its equation.

11. How are the lines alike?

12. How are they different?

13. Adding to *x* does what to the line?

14. Multiplying *x* does what to the line?

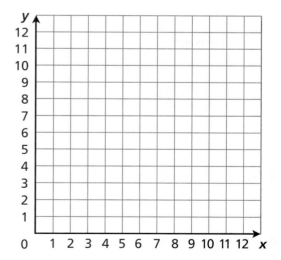

Going Further

▶ Use a Graph to Solve a Problem

Dorothy collected 30 mL of water from a leaking faucet in 2 hours. She wondered about how long it would take to collect 100 mL of water.

Show your work on your Activity Workbook page.

1. Complete the table below to show how much water is collected in 0, 2, and 4 hours.

Time (hr)	0	2	4
Volume of Water (mL)			

2. Graph the points in the table and extend the line. Use the graph to answer the rest of the questions.

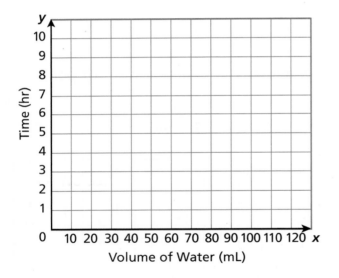

3. How long will it take to collect 90 mL of water?

4. How much water will collect in 8 hours?

5. About how long will it take to collect 100 mL of water?

Graph Functions

Simplify.

1. $2^4 \times 7$

2. $(3 + 2) \times 4 \div 2 - 8$

3. $\sqrt{64}$

4. $\sqrt{144}$

5. Find the value of n that makes this equation true.

$3^n = 243$

$n = $

6. Write the prime factorization of 210. Show your work.

7. Write a situation equation and a solution equation using a variable to represent the unknown.

After the big storm, it took Patrick 9 minutes to clean the snow and ice off each car at the dealership. He worked for 423 minutes. How many cars did he clean?

Situation Equation:

Solution Equation:

Solution:

8. Which values of the variable make the inequality true?

$h - 3 \geq 71$

68   70   74   77   73

9. Complete the rule for the function table. Then write the equation.

Rule in words: Multiply by _____ .						
Equation: _____						
Input (x)	2	3	9	15	21	46
Output (y)	11	13	25	37	49	99

10. **Extended Response** Complete the table and graph the equation to solve the problem.

The phone company charges $3 to change a phone number and $2 to install a new phone jack. When she moved into her new home, Ashley changed her number and had 4 new jacks installed. How much did the phone company charge Ashley for this work?

Number of Phone Jacks Installed	0	1	2		
Cost ($)	$3				

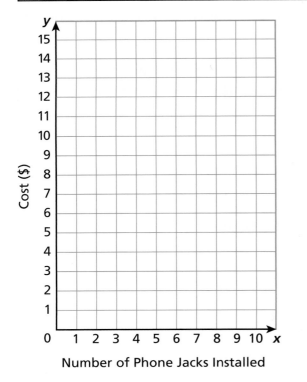

Number of Phone Jacks Installed

Show your work on your Activity Workbook page.

Class Activity

► Fractional Multiplication

Complete.

1. A racetrack is 8 kilometers long. Alex ran around the track 4 times.

   8 taken 4 times = ▢ kilometers

   4 × 8 = ▢ kilometers

2. Kento ran around the same track $\frac{1}{4}$ times.

   8 taken $\frac{1}{4}$ times = ▢ kilometers

   $\frac{1}{4}$ × 8 = ▢ kilometers

3. Markers come in sets of 6. Alta has 3 sets.

   6 taken 3 times = ▢ markers

   3 × 6 = ▢ markers

4. Isabel has $\frac{1}{3}$ of a set of 6 markers.

   6 taken $\frac{1}{3}$ times = ▢ markers

   $\frac{1}{3}$ × 6 = ▢ markers

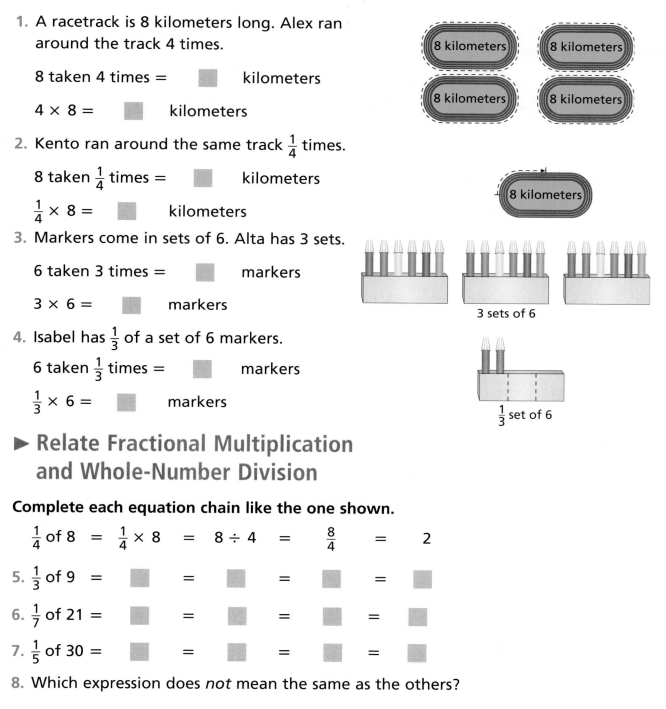

3 sets of 6

$\frac{1}{3}$ set of 6

► Relate Fractional Multiplication and Whole-Number Division

Complete each equation chain like the one shown.

$\frac{1}{4}$ of 8 = $\frac{1}{4}$ × 8 = 8 ÷ 4 = $\frac{8}{4}$ = 2

5. $\frac{1}{3}$ of 9 = ▢ = ▢ = ▢ = ▢

6. $\frac{1}{7}$ of 21 = ▢ = ▢ = ▢ = ▢

7. $\frac{1}{5}$ of 30 = ▢ = ▢ = ▢ = ▢

8. Which expression does *not* mean the same as the others?

   $\frac{1}{6}$ × 24   24 ÷ 6 $\frac{24}{6}$ $\frac{6}{24}$ $\frac{1}{6}$ of 24

▶ Practice with Unit Fractions

9. How many times as many fish did Bill catch as Amy?

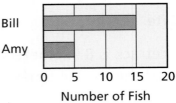

Fish Caught at the Lake

10. How many times as many fish did Amy catch as Bill?

11. What is $\frac{1}{3} \times 15$? What is $15 \div 3$? What is $\frac{15}{3}$?

Write two statements for each pair of players.

12. Compare Gina's points and Brent's points.

Points at the Basketball Game

Player	Points
Gina	32
Brent	8
Jacob	4

13. Compare Brent's points and Jacob's points.

14. Compare Jacob's points and Gina's points.

15. Which are the shortest and longest snakes? How do you know?

Length of Snakes at the Zoo

Snake	Inches
Speedy	n
Lola	$\frac{1}{5} \times n$
Pretzel	$5 \times n$

16. If Speedy is 25 inches long, how long is Lola?

17. If Pretzel is 50 inches long, how long is Speedy? How long is Lola?

Basic Multiplication Concepts

Dear Family,

In this unit of *Math Expressions*, your child is studying multiplication and division with fractions.

Multiplication tells how many times we are taking a number. For example, when we take $\frac{4}{5}$ of something, we multiply it by $\frac{4}{5}$ to find the answer. In this unit, your child will learn to:

• multiply a whole number by a unit fraction

$$\frac{1}{b} \times w = \frac{w}{b}$$ $$\frac{1}{3} \times 5 = \frac{5}{3}$$

• multiply a whole number by a non-unit fraction

$$\frac{a}{b} \times w = \frac{a \times w}{b}$$ $$\frac{2}{3} \times 5 = \frac{10}{3}$$

• multiply two fractions

$$\frac{a}{b} \times \frac{c}{d} = \frac{a \times c}{b \times d}$$ $$\frac{2}{3} \times \frac{5}{7} = \frac{10}{21}$$

Division tells us how many of a certain number are inside another number. For example, when we ask how many times $\frac{4}{5}$ fits inside a number, we divide it by $\frac{4}{5}$ to find out. Using the relationship between multiplication and division, your child will discover how to:

• divide a whole number by a unit fraction

$$w \div \frac{1}{d} = w \times d$$ $$6 \div \frac{1}{5} = 6 \times 5 = 30$$

• divide a unit fraction by a whole number

$$\frac{1}{d} \div w = \frac{1}{d} \times \frac{1}{w}$$ $$\frac{1}{2} \div 4 = \frac{1}{2} \times \frac{1}{4} = \frac{1}{8}$$

• divide a fraction by a fraction

$$\frac{a}{b} \div \frac{c}{d} = \frac{a}{b} \times \frac{d}{c}$$ $$\frac{4}{7} \div \frac{3}{5} = \frac{4}{7} \times \frac{5}{3} = \frac{20}{21}$$

Throughout the unit, students will also practice the fractional operations they have learned previously—comparing, adding, and subtracting. This helps them maintain what they have learned. It also helps them to see how the various fractional operations are alike and how they are different. It is particularly important for your child to realize that comparing, adding, and subtracting fractions require the denominators to be the same. For multiplying and dividing this is not true.

If you have any questions about this unit, please call or write to me.

Sincerely,
Your child's teacher

Your teacher will give you a copy of this letter.

Carta a la familia

Estimada familia:

En esta unidad de *Math Expressions* su niño está estudiando la multiplicación y la división con fracciones.

La multiplicación nos dice cuántas veces se toma un número. Por ejemplo, cuando tomamos $\frac{4}{5}$ de algo, lo multiplicamos por $\frac{4}{5}$ para hallar la respuesta. En esta unidad su niño aprenderá a:

- multiplicar un número entero por una fracción cuyo numerador es uno

$$\frac{1}{b} \times w = \frac{w}{b} \qquad \frac{1}{3} \times 5 = \frac{5}{3}$$

- multiplicar un número entero por una fracción cuyo numerador es diferente de uno

$$\frac{a}{b} \times w = \frac{a \times w}{b} \qquad \frac{2}{3} \times 5 = \frac{10}{3}$$

- multiplicar dos fracciones

$$\frac{a}{b} \times \frac{c}{d} = \frac{a \times c}{b \times d} \qquad \frac{2}{3} \times \frac{5}{7} = \frac{10}{21}$$

La división nos dice qué cantidad de cierto número está dentro de otro número. Por ejemplo, cuando preguntamos cuántas veces cabe $\frac{4}{5}$ en un número, dividimos el número entre $\frac{4}{5}$ para saberlo. Al usar la relación entre la multiplicación y la división, su niño va a descubrir cómo:

- se divide un número entero por una fracción cuyo numerador es uno

$$w \div \frac{1}{d} = w \times d \qquad 6 \div \frac{1}{5} = 6 \times 5 = 30$$

- se divide una fracción cuyo numerador es uno por un número entero

$$\frac{1}{d} \div w = \frac{1}{d} \times \frac{1}{w} \qquad \frac{1}{2} \div 4 = \frac{1}{2} \times \frac{1}{4} = \frac{1}{8}$$

- se divide una fracción entre una fracción

$$\frac{a}{b} \div \frac{c}{d} = \frac{a}{b} \times \frac{d}{c} \qquad \frac{4}{7} \div \frac{3}{5} = \frac{4}{7} \times \frac{5}{3} = \frac{20}{21}$$

> *Tu maestro te dará una copia de esta carta.*

En esta unidad los estudiantes también practicarán las operaciones con fracciones que han aprendido anteriormente: comparaciones, sumas y restas. Esto los ayudará a retener lo que han aprendido. También los ayuda a ver en qué se parecen y en qué se diferencian las operaciones con fracciones. Es importante que su niño se dé cuenta de que para comparar, sumar y restar fracciones, las fracciones deben tener el mismo denominador. En la multiplicación y división esto no se aplica.

Si tiene alguna duda o comentario, por favor comuníquese conmigo.

Atentamente,
El maestro de su niño

Basic Multiplication Concepts

Class Activity

► Visualize the Separate Steps

Silver City is 24 miles away. Gus has driven $\frac{1}{4}$ of the distance. Emma has driven $\frac{3}{4}$ of the distance.

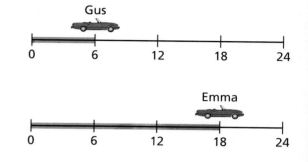

1. How many miles has Gus driven?

2. How many miles has Emma driven?

3. How many times as far as Gus has Emma driven?

4. If $\frac{1}{5}$ of a distance is 3 km, how far is $\frac{4}{5}$?

5. If $\frac{1}{8}$ of a container weighs 2 lbs, how many pounds is $\frac{3}{8}$ of the container?

6. If $\frac{1}{7}$ of a book is 4 pages, how many pages is $\frac{2}{7}$ of the book?

Shady Grove is 40 miles away. Middletown is $\frac{1}{5}$ of the way there and Parkview is $\frac{2}{5}$ of the way.

7. How many miles away is Middletown?

8. How many miles away is Parkview?

9. Ocean City is 42 miles from home. We have gone 35 miles. What fraction of the distance have we gone?

10. Eagle Rock is 72 miles away. When we had gone $\frac{2}{9}$ of the distance, we stopped for gas. How many miles had we traveled?

11. Perilous Peak is 80 miles away. We are $\frac{3}{10}$ of the way there. How many more miles do we have to go?

12. Windy Bay is 48 miles away. Make up your own fraction word problem with multiplication. Be sure to include a non-unit fraction.

▶ Practice Multiplication with Fractions

Solve the problem pairs.

13. $\frac{1}{3}$ of 18 = ▨

 $\frac{2}{3}$ of 18 = ▨

14. $\frac{1}{4} \times 32 = $ ▨

 $\frac{3}{4} \times 32 = $ ▨

15. $\frac{1}{9} \times 27 = $ ▨

 $\frac{4}{9} \times 27 = $ ▨

16. $\frac{1}{6} \times 42 = $ ▨

 $\frac{5}{6} \times 42 = $ ▨

17. Which one does *not* mean the same as the others?

$\frac{2}{3} \times 21$ $\frac{2}{3}$ of 21 $(\frac{1}{3}$ of 21$) + (\frac{1}{3}$ of 21$)$

$\frac{2}{3} + 21$ $\frac{21}{3} + \frac{21}{3}$ $(\frac{1}{3}$ of 21$) \times 2$

Use the table to answer each question.

18. Which building is the tallest? Which is the shortest? How do you know?

Building	Number of Stories
Bank	n
Bus station	$\frac{1}{6} \times n$
Sport shop	$\frac{5}{6} \times n$
Hotel	$6 \times n$

Suppose the bus station is 2 stories tall.

19. How many stories does the sport shop have?

20. How many stories does the bank have?

Suppose the bank is 5 stories tall.

21. How many stories tall is the hotel?

Suppose the hotel is 36 stories tall.

22. How many stories does the bank have?

23. How many stories does the bus station have?

24. How many stories does the sport shop have?

► Visualize Fractional Answers

Farmer Hanson, Farmer Diaz, and Farmer Smith each have 3 acres of land. They each plowed $\frac{1}{5}$ of their land.

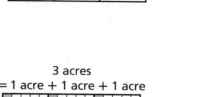

1. Can we tell from the picture how many acres Farmer Hanson plowed? Why or why not?

2. Farmer Smith plowed $\frac{1}{5}$ of each acre. Can we tell from the picture how many acres she plowed? Explain.

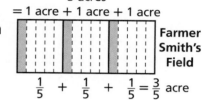

3. How can we tell from Farmer Diaz's field that $\frac{1}{5}$ of each acre added together is the same as $\frac{1}{5}$ of the whole field?

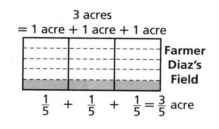

4. Why is $\frac{1}{5}$ of 3 acres the same as $3 \times \frac{1}{5}$ acres?

5. Farmer Belinsky has 7 acres of land. He plowed $\frac{1}{8}$ of each acre. How many acres did he plow altogether?

6. Farmer Davis has 4 acres of land. He plowed $\frac{1}{3}$ of the field. How many acres did he plow?

Solve.

7. Tess practices the flute $\frac{1}{6}$ hour each day. This week she practiced 5 days. How many hours did she practice this week?

Show your work on your paper or in your journal.

Show your work on your Activity Workbook page.

▶ **Multiply by a Non-Unit Fraction**

8. Which one does *not* mean the same as the others?

$\frac{1}{4}$ of 3 $\frac{1}{4} \times 3$ $4 \times \frac{1}{3}$ $\frac{1}{4} + \frac{1}{4} + \frac{1}{4}$ $3 \times \frac{1}{4}$

Circle the fractions on the number lines to help you multiply.

9. $\frac{1}{7} \times 2 = $ ▨

10. $\frac{3}{7} \times 2 = $ ▨

11. $\frac{1}{5} \times 3 = $ ▨

12. $\frac{4}{5} \times 3 = $ ▨

13. $\frac{1}{6} \times 4 = $ ▨

14. $\frac{5}{6} \times 4 = $ ▨

15. $\frac{1}{3} \times 8 = $ ▨

16. $\frac{2}{3} \times 8 = $ ▨

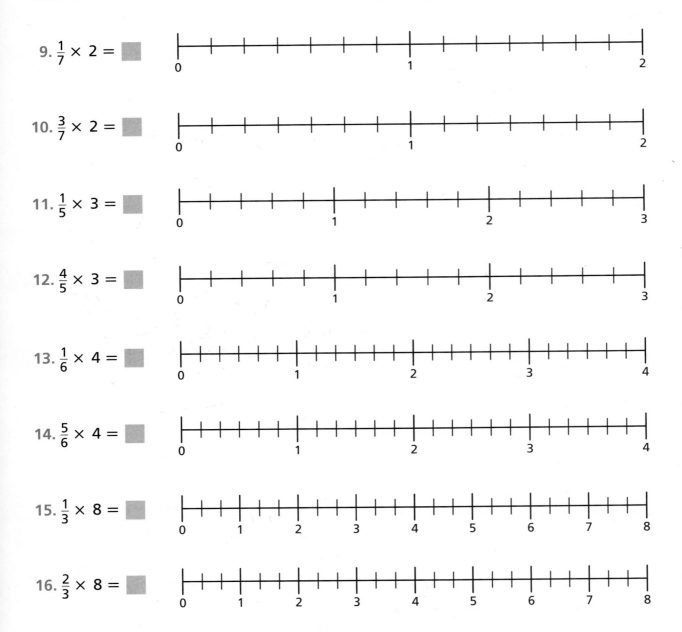

Multiplication with Fractional Solutions

Class Activity

▶ Simplify and Multiply Fractions

Multiply. Simplify first if you can.

1. $\frac{2}{3} \times 30 =$ ▢

2. $\frac{2}{5} \times 35 =$ ▢

3. $\frac{5}{6} \times 4 =$ ▢

4. $\frac{7}{16} \times 8 =$ ▢

5. $\frac{7}{20} \times \frac{5}{14} =$ ▢

6. $\frac{2}{16} \times \frac{4}{21} =$ ▢

7. $\frac{9}{10} \times \frac{7}{10} =$ ▢

8. $\frac{7}{15} \times \frac{10}{21} =$ ▢

9. $\frac{5}{24} \times \frac{6}{25} =$ ▢

10. $\frac{5}{8} \times \frac{32}{45} =$ ▢

11. $\frac{8}{49} \times \frac{7}{10} =$ ▢

12. $\frac{7}{25} \times \frac{3}{4} =$ ▢

13. Which fraction does *not* mean the same as the others?

$\frac{3}{9}$　　　$\frac{1}{3}$　　　$\frac{8}{24}$　　　$\frac{10}{30}$　　　$\frac{6}{18}$　　　$\frac{9}{36}$　　　$\frac{20}{60}$

▶ Problem-Solving Situations

Solve.

Show your work on your paper or in your journal.

14. In the Fireside Ski Shop, $\frac{11}{28}$ of the ski caps have tassels. Of the caps with tassels, $\frac{7}{11}$ are blue. What fraction of the caps in the shop are blue with tassels?

15. In the shop, $\frac{27}{32}$ of the jackets have zippers. Of the jackets with zippers, $\frac{8}{9}$ have hoods. What fraction of the jackets in the shop have both zippers and hoods?

16. Five of the 16 workers in the shop know how to ski. $\frac{1}{5}$ of those who can ski know how to snowboard. What fraction of the workers can ski and snowboard?

▶ Discuss Simplifying to Multiply Fractions

Dear Math Students,

I have a string that is $\frac{3}{4}$ of a yard long. I need to take $\frac{7}{12}$ of it. You can see how I solved the problem at the right.

Now I'm wondering about my answer. When you take a fraction of a fraction, you should get a smaller fraction. But my answer is larger. What mistake did I make? How do I correct it?

Thank you.
Puzzled Penguin

$$\frac{7}{12} \times \frac{3}{4} = \frac{7 \times 3}{\cancel{12 \times 4}} = \frac{21}{3} = 7 \text{ yd}$$
$$3 \times 1$$

I simplified by changing 12×4 to 3×1.

17. Write a response to the Puzzled Penguin.

Multiplication Strategies

▶ Compare Multiplication and Addition

These fraction strips show how we add and multiply fractions.

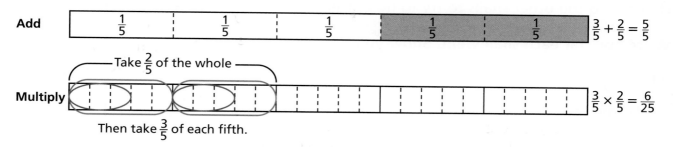

1. Which problem above has the greater answer? How do you know?

2. Tell which of these questions will have the greater answer. Solve each one.

$$\frac{3}{7} + \frac{2}{7} = \blacksquare \qquad \frac{3}{7} \times \frac{2}{7} = \blacksquare$$

3. If the denominators are different, can you still tell which answer will be greater? Write *yes* or *no*. Then solve to check.

$$\frac{3}{4} + \frac{1}{6} = \blacksquare \qquad \frac{3}{4} \times \frac{1}{6} = \blacksquare$$

▶ Compare Fractional and Whole-Number Operations

Tell if each expression has an answer less than or greater than the first number in the expression.

4. $a + b$	**5.** $a - b$	**6.** $a \times b$
7. $\frac{a}{b} + \frac{c}{d}$	**8.** $\frac{a}{b} - \frac{c}{d}$	**9.** $\frac{a}{b} \times \frac{c}{d}$

> *a* and *b* are whole numbers greater than 1.
>
> All of the fractions are less than 1.

10. How is multiplying fractions different from multiplying whole numbers?

Class Activity

Vocabulary
commutative property

▶ Word Problems with Mixed Operations

Amber, a very fit snail, moved $\frac{7}{9}$ yard in an hour. She challenged the other snails to try to do better.

Write how far each snail went. Show your work.

11. Willy moved $\frac{4}{5}$ as far as Amber.

12. Dusty went $\frac{1}{3}$ of a yard less than Amber.

13. Pearl went twice as far as Amber.

14. Casey moved $\frac{4}{9}$ of a yard more than Amber.

15. Minnie moved half as far as Amber.

16. Make up your own question about another snail, Shelly. Ask a classmate to solve it.

▶ The Commutative Property and Fractions

$\frac{a}{b} \times \frac{c}{d} = \frac{c}{d} \times \frac{a}{b}$ This relationship is known as the **commutative property**. Look at the proof below.

$$\frac{a}{b} \times \frac{c}{d} \quad = \quad \frac{a \times c}{b \times d} \quad = \quad \frac{c \times a}{d \times b} \quad = \quad \frac{c}{d} \times \frac{a}{b}$$

Problem   Step 1   Step 2   Step 3

17. Explain why each step is true.

Relate Fractional Operations

▶ Investigate Decimal Patterns

These number lines show decimal equivalents for some common fractions. Discuss patterns you see.

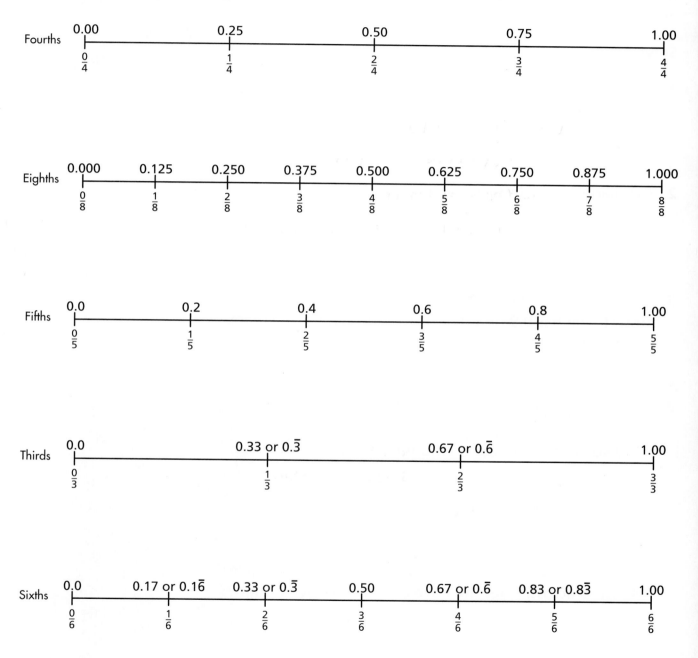

Going Further

▶ Problems with Fractions and Decimals

Some problems use both fractions and decimals. Converting the fractions to decimals can sometimes make it easier to compare or work with the numbers.

Show your work on your paper or in your journal.

Solve.

1. Malcolm made $\frac{2}{7}$ of his free throws this year. His friend Darius made 0.31 of his free throws. Who has a better free-throw record this year?

2. Zoe made $1,000 last year and saved $\frac{7}{8}$ of it. This year she also made $1,000 and saved $890. How much more did she save this year?

3. Berta needs $\frac{7}{8}$ of a pint of whipped cream to make a dessert. She has 0.9 of a pint. How much whipped cream will be left over?

4. The bolts that hold the cables on Trudi's bike measure about 0.12 inches across. She has a set of wrenches in these sizes, measured in fractions of an inch:
$$\frac{5}{32}, \frac{1}{8}, \frac{3}{16}, \frac{1}{4}, \frac{3}{32}.$$

   Which wrench should she use?

5. Trudi also needs to tighten the axle bolts, which measure 0.4 inches across. Does she have a wrench large enough?

Find Decimal Equivalents of Fractions

Class Activity

▶ Explore Fractional Shares

There are 4 people in the Walton family, but there are only
3 waffles. How can the Waltons share the waffles equally?

Divide each waffle into 4 pieces.

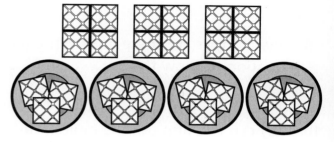

Each person's share of one waffle is $\frac{1}{4}$.
Since there are 3 waffles, each person gets
3 of the $\frac{1}{4}$s, or $\frac{3}{4}$ of a waffle.

$3 \div 4 = 3 \times \frac{1}{4} = \frac{3}{4}$

1. Suppose there are 5 people and 4 waffles.

   What is each person's share of 1 waffle?

   What is each person's share of 4 waffles?

   Complete the equation: $4 \div 5 = $ ▦ $\times$ ▦ $= $ ▦

2. Suppose there are 10 people and 7 waffles.

   What is each person's share of 1 waffle?

   What is each person's share of 7 waffles?

   Complete the equation: $7 \div 10 = $ ▦ $\times$ ▦ $= $ ▦

Complete.

3. $5 \div 6 = $ ▦ $\times$ ▦ $= $ ▦

4. $4 \div 9 = $ ▦ $\times$ ▦ $= $ ▦

Give your answer in the format of an equation.

5. How can you divide 7 waffles equally among 8 people?

6. How can you divide 39 waffles equally among 5 serving plates?

7. Discuss why these equations are true
   for any whole numbers n and d.

   $$n \div d = n \times \underbrace{\frac{1}{d}}_{} = \frac{n}{d}$$

   n unit fractions $\frac{1}{d}$

▶ Divide by a Unit Fraction

8. How many $\frac{1}{8}$s are there in 1? Write a division equation to show this.

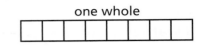

one whole

9. How many $\frac{1}{8}$s are there in 3? Write a division equation to show this.

10. Why can you also use the multiplication equation $3 \times 8 = 24$ to show how many $\frac{1}{8}$s are in 3?

11. How many $\frac{1}{4}$s are there in 5? Write a division and a multiplication equation to show this.

12. Complete the equation. w and d are whole numbers.

$$w \div \frac{1}{d} = \rule{2cm}{0.4pt}$$

Write a division equation. Use multiplication to solve each word problem.

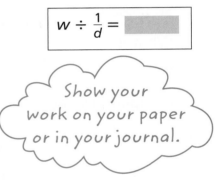

Show your work on your paper or in your journal.

13. Olivia made 9 sandwiches and cut each one into fourths. How many fourths does she have?

14. The 10 members of a hiking club will walk 9 miles. Each person will carry the food pack for an equal distance. How far will each hiker carry the food pack?

15. Damon has a 6-pound bag of cat food. He feeds his cat $\frac{1}{8}$ pound every day. How many days will the bag last?

16. Jodie has a box of 12 chocolates. She and her 7 friends will share them equally. How many chocolates will each person get? Give your answer as a simplified mixed number.

When Dividing Is Also Multiplying

► Unit Fractions in Action

Karen's 5 grandchildren came to visit for 3 days. Karen found a long roll of drawing paper. She said, "I'll cut this paper into 3 equal parts, and we'll use one part on each day." Then she cut the first part into 5 equal parts so each grandchild could make a drawing. She asked her grandchildren, "What part of the whole roll of paper do each of you have? What math problem is this? Make a drawing so Sammy will understand."

Tommy the oldest said, "Today we are using $\frac{1}{3}$ of the whole roll because we have 3 equal parts."

Lucy said, "Then we cut that $\frac{1}{3}$ into 5 equal parts. So we found $\frac{1}{3} \div 5$, a unit fraction divided by the whole number 5."

Asha said, "But we have to divide each of the other two thirds into 5 equal parts to find out how many equal parts we have in all. That's like multiplying by $\frac{1}{5}$!"

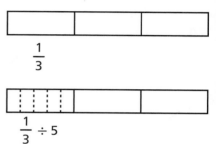

Phoebe said, "Oh look, we have 15 equal parts in all. So today we are each using $\frac{1}{15}$ of the whole roll."

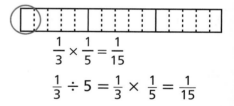

Sammy, the youngest grandchild said, "So dividing by 5 is the same as multiplying by $\frac{1}{5}$ because that also means finding one of five equal parts."

The children said, "So dividing by a whole number w is the same as multiplying by $\frac{1}{w}$."

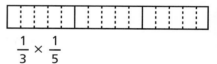

Solve.

17. $\frac{1}{2} \div 3 = \frac{1}{2} \times \boxed{} = \boxed{}$ 18. $\frac{1}{5} \div 2 = \boxed{} \times \boxed{} = \boxed{}$

Class Activity

▶ Practice Divisions

$$n \div d = n \times \frac{1}{d} = \frac{n}{d} \qquad w \div \frac{1}{d} = w \times d \qquad \frac{1}{d} \div w = \frac{1}{d} \times \frac{1}{w} = \frac{1}{d \cdot w}$$

19. Describe patterns you see across these cases.

20. Why is dividing by a whole number the same as multiplying by a unit fraction with that number as its denominator?

21. Why does dividing by a unit fraction make $w \times d$ a larger number?

22. $3 \div 7 = \blacksquare \times \blacksquare = \blacksquare$

23. $5 \div 8 = \blacksquare \times \blacksquare = \blacksquare$

24. $4 \div \frac{1}{3} = \blacksquare \times \blacksquare = \blacksquare$

25. $7 \div \frac{1}{2} = \blacksquare \times \blacksquare = \blacksquare$

26. $\frac{1}{2} \div 5 = \blacksquare \times \blacksquare = \blacksquare$

27. $\frac{1}{3} \div 4 = \blacksquare \times \blacksquare = \blacksquare$

28. For the three expressions below, which answer will be the greatest? the least? in between? Explain.

$$5 \div 3 \qquad \frac{1}{3} \div 5 \qquad 5 \div \frac{1}{3}$$

When Dividing Is Also Multiplying

Class Activity

▶ Add, Subtract, Compare, and Multiply Fractions

The fraction box to the right shows the same two fractions compared, added, subtracted, and multiplied.

Copy and complete the fraction box.

	$\frac{1}{3}$ and $\frac{1}{6}$
>	$\frac{1}{3} > \frac{1}{6}$ or $\frac{2}{6} > \frac{1}{6}$
+	$\frac{1}{3} + \frac{1}{6} = \frac{2}{6} + \frac{1}{6} = \frac{3}{6} = \frac{1}{2}$
−	$\frac{1}{3} - \frac{1}{6} = \frac{2}{6} - \frac{1}{6} = \frac{1}{6}$
×	$\frac{1}{3} \times \frac{1}{6} = \frac{1}{18}$

1.

	$\frac{2}{5}$ and $\frac{7}{10}$
>	
+	
−	
×	

2.

	$\frac{3}{5}$ and $\frac{4}{7}$
>	
+	
−	
×	

3. How are adding, subtracting, and comparing fractions alike?

4. How is multiplication different from the other operations?

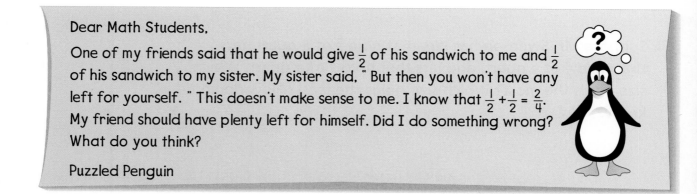

Dear Math Students,

One of my friends said that he would give $\frac{1}{2}$ of his sandwich to me and $\frac{1}{2}$ of his sandwich to my sister. My sister said, " But then you won't have any left for yourself. " This doesn't make sense to me. I know that $\frac{1}{2} + \frac{1}{2} = \frac{2}{4}$. My friend should have plenty left for himself. Did I do something wrong? What do you think?

Puzzled Penguin

5. Write a response to the Puzzled Penguin.

► Word Problems with Mixed Operations

Solve. Answer first in unsimplified form and then in the simplest form.

6. Yesterday Mr. Swenson made $2\frac{3}{4}$ quarts of strawberry jam and $1\frac{1}{8}$ quarts of raspberry jam. How much more strawberry jam did he make than raspberry?

7. Today Mr. Swenson is making $\frac{2}{5}$ of a quart of grape jelly. He will give $\frac{1}{2}$ of this amount to his neighbor. How many quarts will the neighbor get?

8. Mr. Swenson is also making $2\frac{1}{6}$ quarts of cherry jelly and $3\frac{1}{12}$ quarts of orange jelly. He will mix the two kinds together. How much of this mixed jelly will he have?

9. Yesterday Mr. Swenson made $\frac{7}{10}$ of a quart of blueberry jam. His family ate $\frac{1}{10}$ of it. How much of the blueberry jam is left?

10. Suppose Mr. Swenson has jars that hold $\frac{5}{6}$ of a quart, jars that hold $\frac{3}{4}$ of a quart, and jars that hold $\frac{2}{3}$ of a quart. Which size holds the most? Which size holds the least? How do you know?

11. Suppose Mr. Swenson has jars in these sizes:
    $\frac{3}{4}$ quart, $\frac{2}{5}$ quart, $\frac{5}{8}$ quart, $\frac{4}{5}$ quart, $\frac{3}{10}$ quart

    Give the size of these jars in decimal numbers.

Mixed Practice with Fractions

► Divide a Whole Number by a Fraction

Solve. Use the number lines to help you.

A mountain trail is 6 miles long. A group of runners will race to the top of the mountain.

1. The runners expect to see a marker every $\frac{1}{4}$ mile. How many markers will they see? Write the division equation and the answer.

   Think: How many $\frac{1}{4}$s are there in 6? Look at the number line.

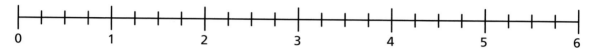

2. The runners expect a water station every $\frac{3}{4}$ mile. Write the division equation and the answer. How many water stations will there be?

   Think: How many $\frac{3}{4}$s are there in 6? Use the number line.

3. How many times as great is your first answer as your second answer? Explain why.

4. Explain why you can solve $6 \div \frac{3}{4}$ in two steps: $6 \times 4 = 24$ and then $24 \div 3 = 8$.

► Divide a Fraction by a Fraction

Solve.

5. Alison has $\frac{2}{3}$ of an hour to write postcards. It takes her $\frac{1}{6}$ of an hour to write each one. How many can she write? Write the division equation and the answer.

Think: How many $\frac{1}{6}$s are in $\frac{2}{3}$? Use the number line.

$\frac{0}{3}$ $\frac{1}{3}$ $\frac{2}{3}$ $\frac{3}{3}$

► Solve Multiplication Equations

Find the unknown factor. Rewrite the equation as a division.

<u>Division Equation</u>

6. $\frac{2}{3} \times \blacksquare = \frac{8}{15}$ $\frac{8}{15} \div \frac{2}{3} = \blacksquare$

7. $\frac{5}{7} \times \blacksquare = \frac{15}{56}$

8. $\frac{5}{6} \times \blacksquare = \frac{15}{24}$

9. $\frac{2}{5} \times \blacksquare = \frac{2}{10}$

10. $\frac{5}{8} \times \blacksquare = \frac{20}{72}$

These products have been simplified. Use the unsimplified fraction to divide.

11. $\frac{2}{5} \times \blacksquare = \frac{6}{20} = \frac{3}{10}$

12. $\frac{3}{4} \times \blacksquare = \frac{15}{24} = \frac{5}{8}$

Show your work on your paper or in your journal.

▶ Unsimplify to Make the Product Divisible

$\frac{2}{3} \div \frac{5}{7} = ?$ We cannot divide the top by 5 or the bottom by 7.

We need to unsimplify $\frac{2}{3}$ so we can divide: $\frac{2}{3} \times \left(\frac{5}{5} \times \frac{7}{7}\right)$

1. Why do you multiply by $\frac{5}{5}$ and $\frac{7}{7}$?

Now let's divide: $\frac{2 \times 5 \times 7}{3 \times 5 \times 7} \div \frac{5}{7} = \frac{(2 \times 5 \times 7) \div 5}{(3 \times 5 \times 7) \div 7}$

2. In the numerator, $5 \div 5 = 1$.
   Divide and write the simplified numerator.

3. In the denominator, $7 \div 7 = 1$.
   Divide and write the simplified denominator.

4. Complete the new equation. $\dfrac{2 \times \blacksquare}{3 \times \blacksquare} = \dfrac{\blacksquare}{\blacksquare}$

5. What happened to the divisor $\frac{5}{7}$ in step 4?

Unsimplify the product to complete each division.

6. $\frac{3}{8} \div \frac{2}{5}$

7. $\frac{4}{9} \div \frac{3}{8}$

8. $\frac{2}{9} \div \frac{3}{10}$

9. $\frac{2}{7} \div \frac{4}{3}$

▶ Understand Division by Inversion

You can unsimplify and divide in one step.

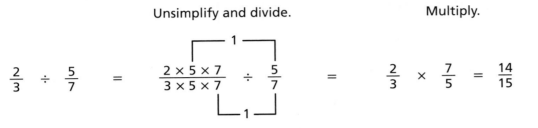

Unsimplify and divide.   Multiply.

$$\frac{2}{3} \div \frac{5}{7} = \frac{2 \times 5 \times 7}{3 \times 5 \times 7} \div \frac{5}{7} = \frac{2}{3} \times \frac{7}{5} = \frac{14}{15}$$

10. How is the final multiplication related to the original division?

11. Complete the algebra equation.

$$\frac{a}{b} \div \frac{c}{d} = \blacksquare \times \blacksquare$$

12. Use the algebra equation to help you divide.

$$\frac{4}{9} \div \frac{3}{5} = \blacksquare$$

13. Solve the equation by unsimplifying the factor.

$$\frac{4}{9} \div \frac{3}{5} = \blacksquare$$

14. What do you notice about the answers to exercises 12 and 13?

▶ Practice Fractional Division

Complete these fractional divisions using any method.

15. $\frac{1}{10} \div \frac{2}{3} = \blacksquare$ 16. $\frac{5}{12} \div \frac{5}{6} = \blacksquare$

17. $\frac{2}{9} \div \frac{3}{4} = \blacksquare$ 18. $2\frac{1}{4} \div \frac{3}{4} = \blacksquare$

19. $\frac{15}{16} \div \frac{5}{4} = \blacksquare$ 20. $\frac{15}{32} \div \frac{3}{4} = \blacksquare$

▶ Solve Fraction Word Problems

The Skyline Skateboard Factory times its workers to see how fast they work. The table shows the time it takes each worker at the factory to make one skateboard. Use the table to solve each problem.

Worker	Time
Kristy	$\frac{3}{5}$ hour
Arturo	$\frac{2}{3}$ hour
Cleta	$\frac{5}{6}$ hour
Tim	$\frac{3}{4}$ hour

Show your work on your paper or in your journal.

Solve.

1. Tim worked for $3\frac{3}{4}$ hours. How many skateboards did he make?

2. Today Kristy worked for $3\frac{1}{3}$ hours. How many skateboards and part-skateboards did she make?

3. Cleta usually works 5 hours a day. How many skateboards and part-skateboards can she make in a day?

4. Yesterday Arturo worked $5\frac{1}{3}$ hours. How many skateboards and part-skateboards did he make?

5. Who is the fastest worker at the Skyline Skateboard Factory?

6. **On the Back** Write a real-world word problem with a solution that involves dividing $3\frac{1}{3}$ by $\frac{3}{5}$. Solve your problem.

Write your answer to the "On the Back" question on your paper or in your journal.

Investigate Division by Inversion

▶ Solve Word Problems with Multiplication and Division

Decide whether you need to multiply or divide. Then solve each problem.

1. A turtle crawls $3\frac{1}{3}$ yards in an hour. How far will it crawl in 2 hours?

   How far will the turtle crawl in $\frac{3}{4}$ of an hour?

2. Emily has $\frac{3}{5}$ of a ton of sand. She will move it by wheelbarrow to the garden. Her wheelbarrow holds $\frac{1}{10}$ of a ton. How many trips will she make?

3. Tawanna runs $2\frac{7}{10}$ miles every day. She stops every $\frac{9}{10}$ of a mile to rest. How many stops does she make?

4. Roberto has a recipe that calls for $\frac{3}{4}$ cup of flour. He wants to use only $\frac{1}{2}$ of the recipe today. How much flour will he need?

5. A picnic jug holds $\frac{5}{8}$ of a gallon of lemonade. Each paper cup holds $\frac{1}{12}$ of a gallon. How many paper cups, and parts of cups, can be filled?

6. On the White Gate Chicken Farm $\frac{7}{8}$ of the eggs usually hatch. This year only $\frac{2}{3}$ as many eggs hatched. What fraction of the eggs hatched this year?

▶ Compare Fractional and Whole-Number Results

In the equations below, a and b are whole numbers greater than 1. $\frac{n}{d}$ is a fraction less than 1. Answer the questions about the equations.

Multiplication

7. $a \times b = c$

   Will c be greater than or less than a? Why?

8. $a \times \frac{n}{d} = c$

   Will c be greater than or less than a? Why?

Division

9. $a \div b = c$

   Will c be greater than or less than a? Why?

10. $a \div \frac{n}{d} = c$

   Will c be greater than or less than a? Why?

Which has the greater answer? Do not try to calculate the answer.

11. $4{,}826 \times 581 \qquad 4{,}826 \div 581$

12. $\frac{27}{83} \times \frac{13}{72} \qquad \frac{27}{83} \div \frac{13}{72}$

▶ Predict the Size of the Result

Decide what operation to use, predict the size of the result, then solve the problem.

13. Lucy spends 4 hours a week baby-sitting. Her sister Lily spends $\frac{7}{8}$ as much time baby-sitting. Does Lily baby-sit for more or less than 4 hours?

    Now find the exact amount of time that Lily baby-sits.

14. Yoshi has a rope 30 feet long. He must cut it into pieces that are each $\frac{5}{6}$ of a foot long. Will he get more or fewer than 30 pieces?

    Now find the exact number of pieces that Yoshi will get.

15. Carlos can throw a ball 14 yards. His friend Raul can throw $\frac{3}{7}$ of that distance. Is Raul's throw longer or shorter than 14 yards?

    Now find the exact length of Raul's throw.

16. An apple orchard covers 12 acres. There is a watering spout for every $\frac{1}{4}$ of an acre. Are there more or fewer than 12 watering spouts?

    Now find the exact number of watering spouts in the orchard.

▶ Summarize Fractional Operations

17. You have just won a prize on a new quiz show called *Quick Thinking*. The prize will be *n* CDs from your favorite music store. You also have a chance to change your prize if you think you can make it better. The screen shows the other choices that you have. Which one will you choose?

18. Suppose that *n* = 6. How many CDs have you won?

19. Suppose that *n* = 12. How many CDs have you won?

20. Summarize what you have learned about the size of the answers when you mulitiply and divide by whole numbers and by fractions.

Show your work on your paper or in your journal.

Distinguish Multiplication from Division

▶ Choose the Operation

Decide what operation to use. Then solve. Simplify your answers.

1. Hala can ride her bike $7\frac{1}{2}$ miles in an hour. How far will she ride in 3 hours? How far will she ride in $\frac{2}{3}$ of an hour?

2. Eryn's pet rabbit eats $\frac{5}{12}$ of a pound of food every day. If Eryn buys rabbit food in 5-pound bags, how often does she buy a new bag of rabbit food?

3. Jason practices the trumpet for $1\frac{2}{3}$ hours every day. He practices the scales every $\frac{1}{3}$ of an hour. How many times does he practice the scales?

4. Jonathan can throw a baseball $10\frac{1}{3}$ yards. His brother Joey can throw a baseball $13\frac{1}{12}$ yards. How much farther can Joey throw the ball?

5. Kim bought $\frac{3}{8}$ of a pound of sunflower seeds and $\frac{3}{16}$ of a pound of thistle seed for her bird feeder. How much seed did she buy in all?

6. Casandra's fish bowl holds $\frac{9}{10}$ gallon of water. It is now $\frac{2}{3}$ full. How much water does it have?

> Show your work on your paper or in your journal.

▶ Estimate Answers

7. Marcus plays basketball for 9 hours each week. His friend Luis spends $\frac{5}{6}$ as much time playing basketball. Who plays more basketball?

8. How much time does Luis spend playing basketball?

9. Stacey's long jump is 10 feet. That is $\frac{5}{6}$ of a foot longer than Ron's jump. Does Ron jump more or less than 10 feet?

10. How long was Ron's jump?

▶ Practice Fractional Operations

Write the answer in simplest form.

11. $\frac{7}{15} \div \frac{2}{3} = $ ▨

12. $\frac{5}{12} \div \frac{3}{8} = $ ▨

13. $\frac{1}{8} + \frac{5}{6} = $ ▨

14. $\frac{4}{9} \div 8 = $ ▨

15. $\frac{4}{7} - \frac{1}{3} = $ ▨

16. $\frac{5}{8} \times \frac{5}{12} = $ ▨

17. $\frac{3}{5} - \frac{6}{35} = $ ▨

18. $\frac{2}{5} \times 5 = $ ▨

19. $\frac{1}{6} + \frac{2}{9} = $ ▨

20. $\frac{2}{3} - \frac{1}{12} = $ ▨

21. $\frac{7}{8} \times \frac{2}{5} = $ ▨

22. $3 - \frac{4}{5} = $ ▨

▶ Summarize

a is a whole number greater than 1.

$\frac{n}{d}$ is a fraction less than 1.

Write whether c is greater than (>) or less than (<) a.

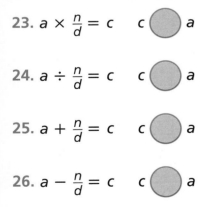

23. $a \times \frac{n}{d} = c$ c ◯ a

24. $a \div \frac{n}{d} = c$ c ◯ a

25. $a + \frac{n}{d} = c$ c ◯ a

26. $a - \frac{n}{d} = c$ c ◯ a

9–14
Class Activity

▶ Problems Involving Means

The mean (average) of a data set is the equal group that describes the data set. To find it:

- Add all of the numbers in the data set.

- Divide the total by the number of items in the data set.

$$\begin{array}{r} 3.5 \\ 3.25 \\ 4.125 \\ 4 \\ +\ 3.4 \\ \hline 18.275 \end{array}$$

Tyra is training for a race. She ran these distances last week:

$3\frac{1}{2}$ miles, $3\frac{1}{4}$ miles, $4\frac{1}{8}$ miles, 4 miles, and $3\frac{2}{5}$ miles. To find the mean, she wrote all the fractions in decimal form and then added them and divided by 5. Tyra's mean training distance was 3.655 miles.

$$5\overline{)18.275}^{\,3.655}$$

Solve. Change fractions to decimals if it is easier.

27. Tyra drinks a lot of water on the day of a race. At the last race she drank $1\frac{1}{2}$ cups, $1\frac{7}{8}$ cups, and $3\frac{3}{4}$ cups. What was the mean amount of water that Tyra drank?

Show your work on your paper or in your journal.

28. Sam works at a deli counter. His boss asked him to find the mean weight of the next four customer orders. The orders were: $1\frac{1}{4}$ pounds of ham, $1\frac{1}{2}$ pounds of cheese, 2 pounds of turkey, and $2\frac{3}{4}$ pounds of roast beef. What was the mean weight? Try to solve this with fractions.

29. Tony and his friends sold snacks at the school play to raise money for the Drama Club. They collected $12.50 for muffins, $3.75 for apples, $5.60 for juice, $12.50 for pretzels, $16.00 for yogurt, and $1.40 for carrot sticks. What was the mean amount of money collected to the nearest cent?

30. **On the Back** Write a real-world problem with a solution that involves finding the mean. Explain how to solve the problem.

Write your answer to the "On the Back" question on your paper or in your journal.

Review Operations with Fractions

▶ Math and Construction

A geodesic dome structure is made up of triangles. The more triangles that are used, the closer the structure resembles a sphere. The most popular shape for a geodesic dome is based on an icosahedron, a 3-dimensional shape having 20 triangular faces.

Buildings constructed of triangles are very strong. Dome buildings are spacious, strong, save energy, and use fewer materials to build. Many manufacturers offer kits to build small dome shelters, garages, homes, or storage areas.

1. Len builds a geodesic dome shed that is 12 ft 7 in. across and 6 ft 3 in. high. What are the width and height in feet? Use a mixed number.

   What are the width and height in inches?

2. Len's geodesic dome has parts fastened together with nuts, bolts, and washers. Len needs 100 1-inch long bolts that cost $0.19 each. Excluding tax, how much will he pay for these bolts?

3. Len's dome requires 45 triangles. Thirty of them are $35\frac{3}{8}$ inches tall and 48 inches wide. What is the total area covered by the 30 triangles?

4. A large dome house usually has triangular or hexagonal-shaped skylight windows. One house design has 5 hexagonal windows with sides 24 inches long. Inside the house, these windows are trimmed around the edges with wood. If the trim costs $1.88 per foot, what is the approximate total cost of the wood trim?

► Which Shapes Make Tessellations?

A **tessellation** is a pattern of repetitions that cover a flat surface so there are no gaps or overlaps. Three regular polygons—equilateral triangles, squares, and regular hexagons—make single-shape tessellations like those shown at the right. You can also make tessellations with more than one type of shape.

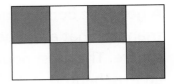

Cut out each shape from Polygons (TRB M88). Trace around the shapes to try to make single-shape tessellations.

5. Do regular pentagons tesselate? Explain.

6. Do the triangles make tessellations?

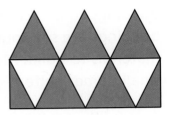

7. Do the quadrilaterals tessellate?

8. Study your tessellations. What do you notice about the angles around any point in the tessellations you were able to make?

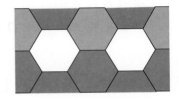

9. Make a conjecture about how you can tell if a shape with 4 or more sides tessellates without trying to create the tessellation.

   My conjecture is:

10. Use a protractor and your cut-out shapes to see if your conjecture is true. What is your conclusion?

11. Try to draw a hexagon that does not tessellate. Explain why you can or cannot.

12. Try to draw a pentagon that does tessellate. Explain why you can or cannot.

Use Mathematical Processes

Solve. Show your work.

1. $\frac{1}{5} \times 2 =$ ▨

2. $\frac{3}{5} \times 2 =$ ▨

3. $\frac{1}{5} \times 20 =$ ▨

4. $\frac{2}{3} \times 30 =$ ▨

5. $\frac{3}{4} \times \frac{2}{5} =$ ▨

6. $\frac{2}{3} \times \frac{6}{10} =$ ▨

7. Todd worked in the garden for $\frac{3}{4}$ of an hour. He spent $\frac{1}{4}$ of that time digging weeds. How long did he dig weeds?

Give the decimal equivalent.

8. $\frac{1}{8} =$ ▨

9. $\frac{3}{4} =$ ▨

Give the fraction equivalent.

10. $0.\overline{3} =$ ▨

11. $0.8 =$ ▨

12. How is multiplying fractions different from adding and subtracting them?

Solve. Show your work.

13. $3 \div 5 =$ ▨

14. $3 \div \frac{1}{5} =$ ▨

15. $3 \div \frac{2}{5} =$ ▨

16. $\frac{8}{9} \div \frac{2}{3} =$ ▨

17. $\frac{3}{7} \div \frac{4}{5} =$ ▨

18. $\frac{1}{3} \div 9 =$ ▨

19. Find the mean of this set of data:

$$\frac{2}{3} \quad \frac{2}{9} \quad \frac{1}{3} \quad \frac{5}{6} \quad \frac{1}{2} \quad \frac{4}{9}$$

20. **Extended Response** Will $4 \div \frac{2}{3}$ be greater or less than 4? Explain why.

Class Activity

▶ Repeating Patterns

1. What are the repeating terms of the pattern?

2. How many times does the pattern repeat?

Use the pattern below to solve exercises 3–4.

3. Draw the repeating terms of the pattern.

4. Will the next term in the repeating pattern be an arrow pointing down? Explain.

Use the pattern below to solve exercises 5–6.

5. Show one way to extend the pattern. Draw the next three terms.

6. Show another way to extend the pattern. Draw the next three terms.

▶ Describe and Extend Growing Patterns

Use the pattern to solve exercises 7–10.

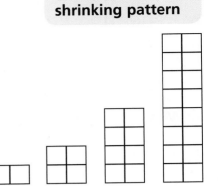

7. What type of pattern is this? How do you know?

8. How does each figure in the pattern change from one term to the next?

9. Describe the next figure in the pattern.

10. What rule could you use to predict the number of squares for any term in the pattern?

▶ Describe and Extend Shrinking Patterns

Use the pattern below to solve exercises 11–13.

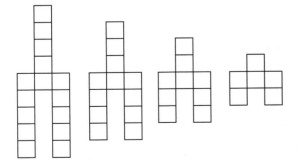

11. What type of pattern is this? How do you know?

12. What rule describes the pattern?

13. Draw the next figure in the pattern.

Dear Family,

In our math class, we are studying patterns and transformations. Your child will work first with geometric patterns and then with number patterns. Your child will apply the four operations—addition, subtraction, multiplication, and division to describe, extend, and make generalizations about growing and shrinking patterns. Examples of patterns are shown below.

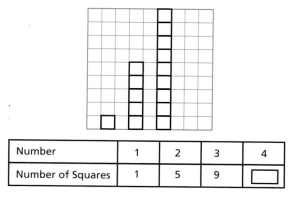

Number	1	2	3	4
Number of Squares	1	5	9	

In addition, your child will explore congruence and patterns of transformations in the coordinate plane. Changing the position of a shape is called a *transformation*. Examples of transformations are shown below.

Transformations

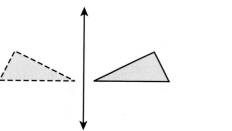

Rotation
(turn)

Reflection
(flip)

Translation
(slide)

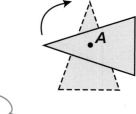

The grid shows a translation of triangle *ABC*: each point of the triangle has been moved two units to the right and one unit up.

If you have any questions or comments, please call or write to me.

Sincerely,
Your child's teacher

Estimada familia:

En nuestra clase de matemáticas estamos estudiando patrones y transformaciones. Su hijo/a comenzará trabajando con patrones geométricos y luego seguirá con patrones numéricos. Su hijo/a aplicará las cuatro operaciones, suma, resta, multiplicación y división, para describir, ampliar y hacer generalizaciones sobre patrones crecientes y decrecientes.

A continuación mostramos ejemplos de patrones.

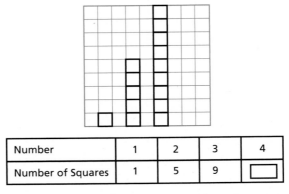

Number	1	2	3	4
Number of Squares	1	5	9	

Además, su hijo/a explorará la congruencia y los patrones de transformación en el plano de coordenadas. Una transformación es el cambio de posición de una figura. A continuación mostramos ejemplos de transformaciones.

Transformations

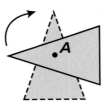

Rotation
(turn)

Reflection
(flip)

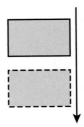

Translation
(slide)

Tu maestro te dará una copia de esta carta.

La cuadrícula muestra la traslación del triángulo ABC: cada punto del triángulo se ha movido dos unidades hacia la derecha y una unidad hacia arriba.

Si tiene alguna pregunta o comentario, por favor comuníquese conmigo.

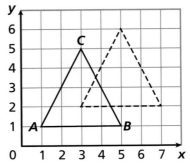

Atentamente,
El maestro de su niño

▶ Numerical Patterns

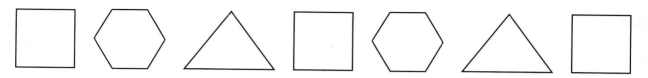

1. How many sides does each figure have?

2. What are the repeating terms in the numerical pattern?

3. What is the next term in the numerical pattern?

Study the pattern. Then answer the questions.

4. $\frac{3}{8}, \frac{8}{3}, \frac{3}{8}, \frac{8}{3}, \frac{3}{8}, \frac{8}{3}, \frac{3}{8}, \frac{8}{3}, \frac{3}{8}, \cdots$

   a. What are the repeating terms in the pattern?

   b. What is the next term in the pattern?

5. 0.1, 0.5, 0.1, 0.1, 0.5, 0.1, 0.1, 0.5, 0.1, …

   a. How many terms repeat in the pattern?

   b. What is the next term in the pattern? How did you find the answer?

▶ Extend a Sequence More Than One Way

Show two different ways to extend the pattern.

6. 8, 2, 8, …

7. 9, 9, 4, 9, 9, …

Show your work on your paper or in your journal.

▶ Growing and Shrinking Patterns

Make a drawing to solve.

8. Students wash 4 cars during the first hour of a car wash. They wash 8 cars the second hour, 12 cars the third hour, and 16 cars the fourth hour. If the pattern continues for 2 more hours, how many cars will students wash in all?

Write an equation to represent the function. Then copy and complete the table.

9.

n	1	2	3	4	5
p	6	12	18	24	▩

10.

x	1	2	3	4	5
y	5	8	11	14	▩

11.

r	40	35	30	25	20
s	8	7	6	5	▩

12.

a	32	30	28	26	24
b	13	12	11	10	▩

Solve.

13. Lisa wrote the equation $m = k \div 4$ to show m as a function of k in the table below. What is wrong with her equation? Write the correct equation.

k	48	44	40	36	32
m	10	9	8	7	▩

▶ Discuss Rotations

Vocabulary

rotation
reflection

You can rotate, or turn, a figure clockwise or counterclockwise about a point. The **rotation**, or movement of the figure, is measured in degrees (°). Each triangle below shows the result of a 90° counterclockwise rotation about point A, when point A is

inside the triangle.   on the triangle.   outside the triangle.

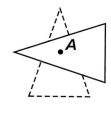
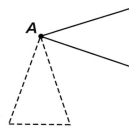
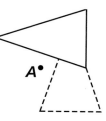

1. Cut out the figures on Activity Workbook page 123. Work with a partner to show clockwise and counterclockwise rotations of 90°, 180°, and 270°.

2. Look at two consecutive figures in the pattern below. How many degrees has the figure been rotated?

3. Draw the fifteenth figure in the pattern.

▶ Discuss Reflections

You can reflect, or flip, a figure across a line. The line is called the line of **reflection**.

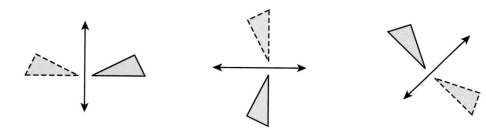

4. **On the Back** Use the figures you cut out and Grid Paper to show a reflection across a line for each figure.

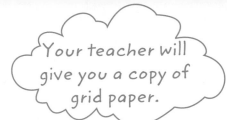

▶ Grid Paper

Your teacher will give you a copy of grid paper.

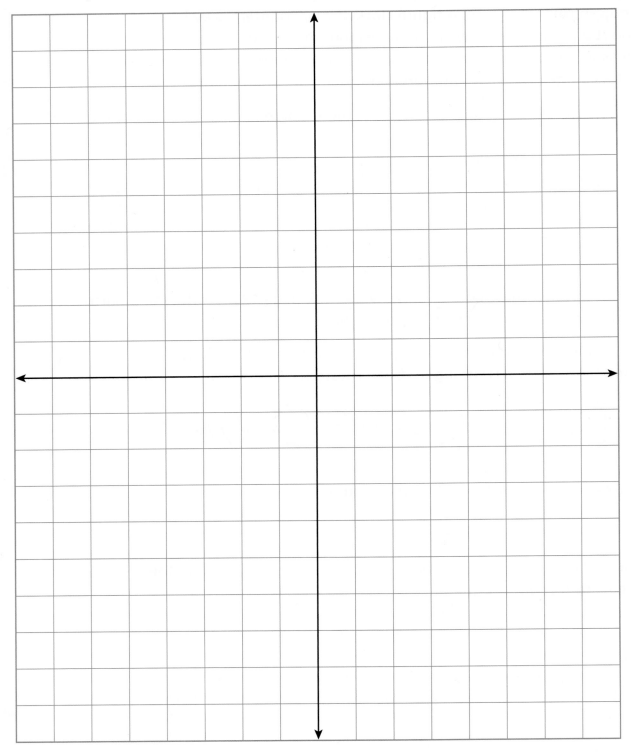

Explore Transformations

▶ Discuss Translations

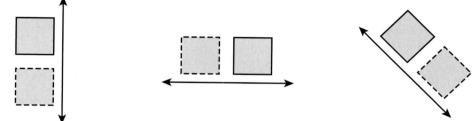

A **translation** is a slide. When a figure is translated, each of its points moves the same distance in the same direction. These squares have been translated along the lines.

5. Use the figures you cut out and Grid Paper to show a translation along a horizontal line for each figure.

▶ Draw Transformations

Draw each transformation on grid paper.

6. a reflection across the line

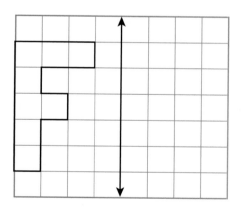

7. a translation along the line

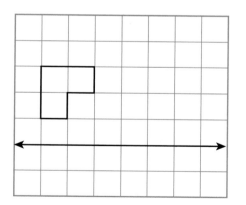

Draw the figure that comes next in the sequence.

8.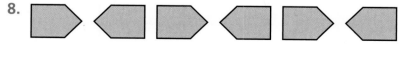

9.

Your teacher will give you a copy of grid paper.

▶ **Grid Paper**

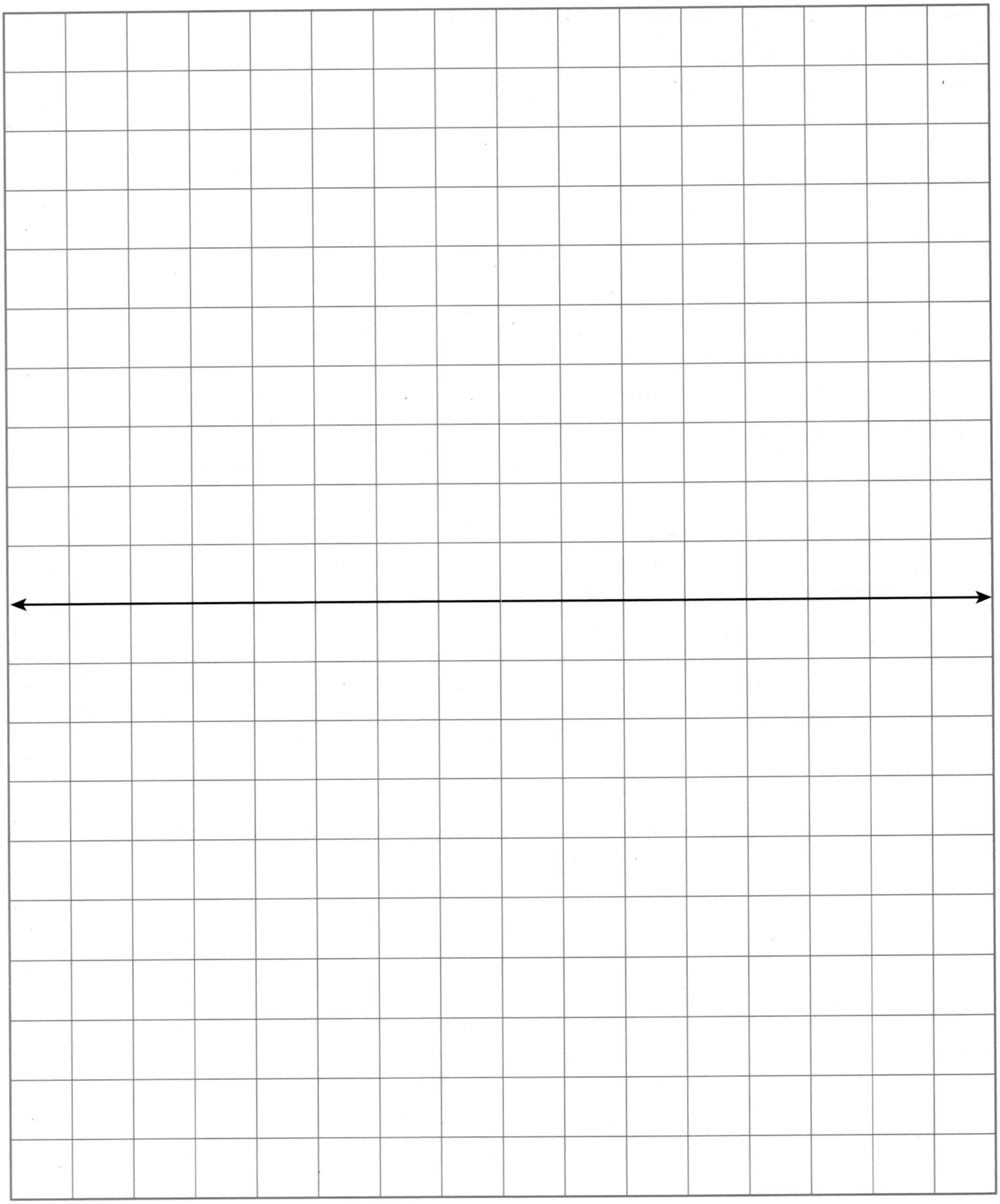

Explore Transformations

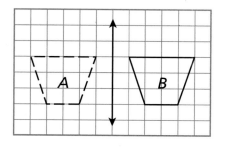

Show your work on your paper or in your journal.

Vocabulary

transformation
congruent

▶ Transformations and Congruence

You have explored three **transformations**, or changes in the position of a figure.

Will a rotation, reflection, or translation of a figure always produce an image that is congruent to the original figure? Remember, two figures are **congruent** when they are exactly the same size and shape.

10. Will the reflection of Figure *A* across a line produce a congruent figure? Make a drawing to prove your answer.

Draw a congruent figure on grid paper, using the transformation given.

11. reflection

12. rotation

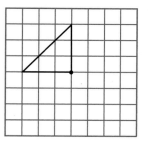

13. translation

14. 180° rotation

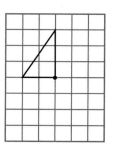

Going Further

Show your work on your paper or in your journal.

▶ Patterns and Transformations

Repeating patterns can often be described by transformations. In the pattern below, the number 3 reflects across a vertical line.

3Ɛ3Ɛ3

For each pattern below, use *rotation, reflection,* or *translation* to describe the rule. Draw the figure that comes next in the series.

1. L L ⊐L L ⊐L L

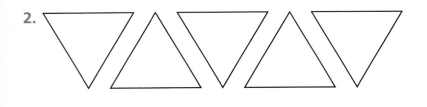

2.

3.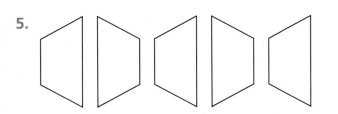

4.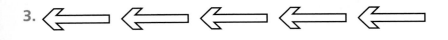

5.

Explore Transformations

▶ Translate Figures in the Coordinate Plane

To translate a figure means to slide it to a different place. On the graph, triangle *PQR* has been translated to the right.

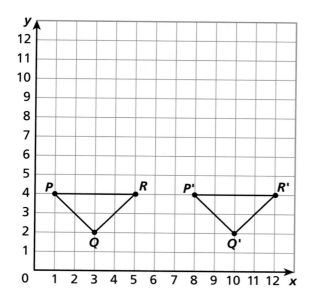

Show your work on your Activity Workbook page.

Complete.

1. The distance from *P* to *P'* is _____ units.

2. The distance from *Q* to *Q'* is _____ units.

3. The distance from *R* to *R'* is _____ units.

4. Triangle *P'Q'R'* has been translated _____ units. The distance between each pair of corresponding points is _____ units.

5. Translate each point of triangle *PQR* up 5 units on the coordinate grid above. Use a ruler to draw the new triangle.

6. Where are the vertices of the second translated triangle?

   (_____, _____) (_____, _____) (_____, _____)

7. What is the numerical relationship between the coordinates for *PQR* and its translated coordinates in exercise 6? Why?

Class Activity

▶ Reflect Figures in the Coordinate Plane

When a figure is reflected, each of its corresponding points is exactly the same distance from the line of reflection.

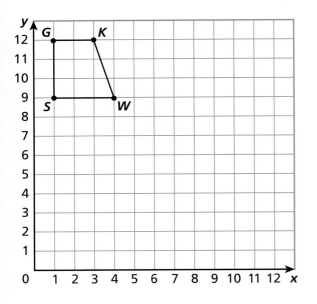

> *Show your work on your Activity Workbook page.*

8. Plot a point at (6, 9) and plot a point at (6, 12). Using your ruler, draw a line through the points.

9. Reflect trapezoid *GKWS* across the line you drew for exercise 8. Where are the vertices of the reflected trapezoid?

   (_____, _____) (_____, _____) (_____, _____) (_____, _____)

10. Plot points at (1, 6) and (4, 6). Using your ruler, draw a line through the points.

11. Reflect trapezoid *GKWS* across the line you drew for exercise 10. Where are the vertices of the reflected trapezoid?

   (_____, _____) (_____, _____) (_____, _____) (_____, _____)

12. Discuss the numerical relationship between the coordinates for trapezoid *GKWS* and the coordinates of the reflections in exercises 9 and 11. Explain your thinking.

Show your work on your Activity Workbook page.

▶ Combinations of Transformations

You can use more than one transformation to move a figure in the coordinate plane.

1. Translate rectangle *BCDE* right 6 units.

2. Where are the vertices of the translated rectangle?

   (_____, _____) (_____, _____)

   (_____, _____) (_____, _____)

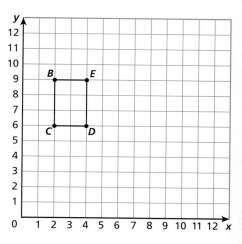

3. Plot points (8, 5) and (10, 5). Using your ruler, draw a line through the points.

4. Reflect rectangle *BCDE* across the line you drew in exercise 3. What are the vertices of the reflected rectangle?

   (_____, _____) (_____, _____)

   (_____, _____) (_____, _____)

5. Reflect triangle *WXY* across the line.

6. Where are the vertices of the reflected triangle?

   (_____, _____) (_____, _____)

   (_____, _____)

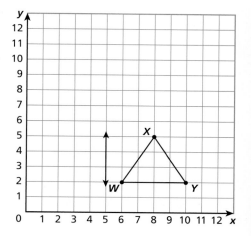

7. Translate triangle *WXY* up 4 units.

8. Where are the vertices of the translated triangle?

   (_____, _____) (_____, _____)

   (_____, _____)

9. **On the Back** Make your own design using two different polygons and combinations of reflections and translations.

Transformations in the Coordinate Plane

1. Show two different ways to extend the pattern. Draw the next three terms for each pattern.

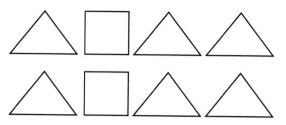

Use the pattern below to solve exercises 2–4.

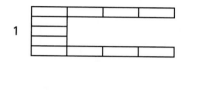

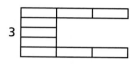

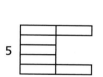

2. What type of pattern is this? How do you know?

3. What is the rule for this pattern?

4. Draw the next term of the pattern above.

5. Show two different ways to extend this numerical pattern.

$$\frac{1}{8}, \frac{1}{4}, \frac{1}{8}$$

$$\frac{1}{8}, \frac{1}{4}, \frac{1}{8}$$

6. Write an equation to represent the function. Then complete the table.

c	1	2	3	4	5
d	6	8	10	12	

7. Describe the transformation that resulted in triangle X′Y′Z′.

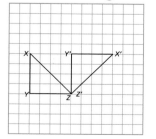

Show your work on your Activity Workbook page.

8. What do you know about the numerical relationship between the coordinates for parallelogram *PQRS* and the coordinates for parallelogram *P'Q'R'S'*?

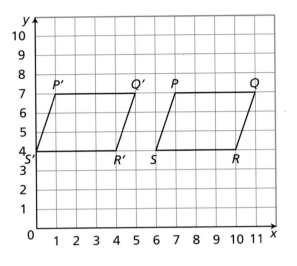

9. Reflect the rectangle across the given line. Where are the vertices of the reflected rectangle?

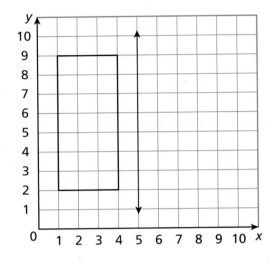

10. **Extended Response** Plot the points (1, 8) and (15, 8). Use your ruler to draw a line through the points. Draw a rectangle with vertices (4, 3), (4, 5), (11, 3), and (11, 5). Reflect the rectangle over the line you drew, and record the vertices.

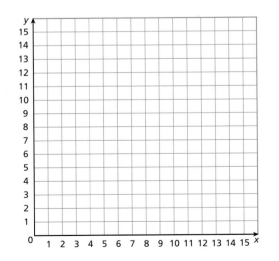

▶ Find the Total So Far

Noreen started to save money. Every day she put three $1 coins into her duck bank. Write how much money she had each day.

On Day 0 Noreen did not put money into her duck bank.		On Day 0 Noreen's duck bank was empty. She had $0.
1. On Day 1 Noreen put $3 into her bank.		On Day 1 Noreen had $_____ in her bank.
2. On Day 2 Noreen put $3 into her bank.		On Day 2 Noreen had $_____ in her bank.
3. On Day 3 Noreen put $3 into her bank.		On Day 3 Noreen had $_____ in her bank.
4. On Day 4 Noreen put $3 into her bank.		On Day 4 Noreen had $_____ in her bank.
5. On Day 5 Noreen put $3 into her bank.		On Day 5 Noreen had $_____ in her bank.
6. On Day 6 Noreen put $3 into her bank.		On Day 6 Noreen had $_____ in her bank.

7. **On the Back** Draw and write how much money Noreen would have in her bank on Day 7 and on Day 8.

Multiplication Patterns

Vocabulary

Multiplication
Column Table

► Complete a Multiplication Column Table

This **Multiplication Column Table** shows Noreen's savings.

8. Fill in the rest of the table to show how much money Noreen saved each day and how much her total was each day.

Days	Dollars	
0	0	
1	3	+3
2		
3		

Write your answers on your paper or in your Activity Workbook.

9. What did you write beside each column?

10. What does the number beside each column show?

► Identify Multiplication Column Tables

These tables show four different ways Noreen could have saved money. Complete each table. Then decide which tables are Multiplication Column Tables and which are not. Explain why.

11.

Days	Dollars	
0	0	
1	2	+2
2		+2
3		+2
4		+2
5		+2
6		+2

Class Activity

Write your answers on your paper or in your Activity Workbook.

12.

Days	Dollars
0	0
1	4
2	12
3	18
4	20
5	24
6	28

+4

13.

Days	Dollars
0	0
1	7
2	14
3	21
4	28
5	35
6	42

14.

Days	Dollars
0	0
1	3
2	5
3	5
4	9
5	11
6	14

Multiplication Patterns

Dear Family,

In our math class, we are exploring the ideas of ratio and proportion.

The ratio of one number to another is a simple way to express the relative size of two quantities or measurements. For example, the ratio of the lengths of the sides of this rectangle is 3 to 2.

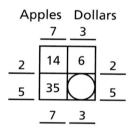

2 in.

3 in.

A proportion is an equation that shows two equivalent ratios. It can be written $14 : 6 = 35 : 15$ or $14 : 6 : : 35 : 15$.

Here is a proportion problem:
Grandfather bought 14 apples for $6. If I buy the same kind of apples, how much will 35 apples cost?

The problem makes this proportion:

$$14 : 6 = 35 : c$$

To solve it, we can put the ratios in a Factor Puzzle like your child has been solving all year.

$$c \text{ is } 3 \times 5 = 15$$

The Factor Puzzle is from the rows of the ratio table that are ×2 and ×5 of the basic ratio 7 : 3. Factor Puzzles enable your child to understand and solve challenging proportion problems.

Ratio Table

Apples	Dollars	
7	3	
0	0	
+7 →	7	3	← +3
+7 →	14	6	← +3
+7 →	21	18	← +3
+7 →	28	24	← +3
+7 →	35	30	← +3
+7 →	42	36	← +3

Discuss with your child any proportions you use in your life, such as doubling a recipe.

If you have any questions, please call or write to me.

Sincerely,
Your child's teacher

Your teacher will give you a copy of this letter.

Estimada familia:

En la clase de matemáticas estamos explorando las razones y las proporciones.

La razón de un número a otro es una manera simple de expresar el tamaño relativo de dos cantidades o medidas. Por ejemplo, la razón de las longitudes de los lados de este rectángulo es de 3 a 2.

2 pulg

3 pulg

Una proporción es una ecuación que muestra 2 razones equivalentes. Se puede escribir $14 : 6 = 35 : 15$ ó $14 : 6 : : 35 : 15$

Éste es un problema de proporción:
El abuelo compró 14 manzanas con $6.
Si compro el mismo tipo de manzanas,
¿cuánto costarán 35 manzanas?

El problema hace esta proporción:

$$14 : 6 = 35 : c$$

Para resolverlo, podemos poner las razones en un rompecabezas de factores como los que su niño ha resuelto durante el año.

c es $3 \times 5 = 15$

Manzanas Dólares

	7	3	
2	14	6	2
5	35	◯	5
	7	3	

El rompecabezas de factores se forma con las filas de la tabla de razones que son × 2 y × 5 de la razón básica 7 : 3. Los rompecabezas de factores ayudan a su niño a comprender y resolver problemas complicados de proporciones.

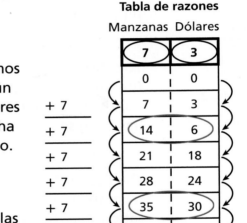

Tabla de razones

Manzanas Dólares

	7	3	
	0	0	
+ 7	7	3	+ 3
+ 7	14	6	+ 3
+ 7	21	18	+ 3
+ 7	28	24	+ 3
+ 7	35	30	+ 3
+ 7	42	36	+ 3

Comente con su niño cualquier tipo de proporciones que usen en la vida diaria, tales como duplicar una receta de cocina.

Si tiene preguntas, por favor comuníquese conmigo.

Atentamente,
El maestro de su niño

Tu maestro te dará una copia de esta carta.

Multiplication Patterns

11–2

Class Activity

▶ Use Unit Rate Language

Write each phrase in your own words. Do not use *per*.

1. 7 days *per* week

2. 9 feet *per* second

3. 9 books *per* shelf

4. $7 *per* sack of rice

▶ Use Different Units and Groups

Every Multiplication Column Situation is divided into **units**, and describes a constant group for each unit. Which of these are Multiplication Column Situations? For each one:

• tell the unit and group per unit

• write the situation using the word *per*.

5. In the zoo, 7 kangaroos live in each of the kangaroo living areas.

6. The band marched on the field one row at a time. There were six people in every row.

7. Pedro and Pilar collect snails. Each day they add 4 snails to their terrarium.

8. Last week Ben saw 3 films, this week he saw 4 films, and next week he will see 2 films.

Write your answers on your paper or in your Activity Workbook.

9. A hot-air balloon is rising up from the school baseball field. It rises 9 feet every second.

10. A bagging machine was set to place the same number of oranges in each bag. Today none of the settings stay fixed. The machine places 3 and then 5 and then 9 oranges in bags.

11. Every day this week Joanne made 3 of her 7 free throws during basketball practice.

12. Sandy loves crossword puzzles. She can solve 8 clues each minute.

13. Farmer Brown is driving his tractor down his hilly and flat fields. He can plough 7 rows per hour on the flat field. On the hilly field he sometimes ploughs 6 and sometimes only 5 rows each hour.

Make a Multiplication Column Table for the situations in exercises 5 and 6.

14.

Unit	Rate
Living Area	**Kangaroos**
0	

+ ▦
+ ▦
+ ▦
+ ▦
+ ▦
+ ▦

15.

Unit	Rate
Rows	**People**
0	

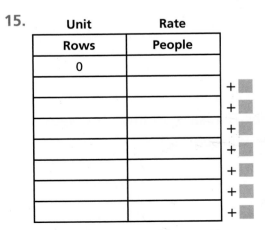

Unit Rate

▶ Describe a Multiplication Column Situation

Decide if each situation is a Multiplication Column Situation.
Write the unit and group for stories that are Multiplication
Column Situations. Write *no* if it is not a Multiplication
Column Situation.

1. Each fish tank has 4 snails to help keep the tanks clean.

   Unit: ▢

   Group (the unit rate): ▢

2. Everyone in the Green family had 2 eggs for breakfast yesterday

   Unit: ▢

   Group (the unit rate): ▢

3. Tara makes 9 drawings on each page of her sketchbook.

   Unit: ▢

   Group: ▢

4. Erin puts 3 large photos on 1 shelf and 7 small photos on 1 shelf.

   Unit: ▢

   Group: ▢

5. Jonathan saves $8 every week, but last week he spent some of
   his savings to go to a movie.

   Unit: ▢

   Group: ▢

6. Fred planted 7 tomato vines in each yard he takes care of.

   Unit: ▢

   Group: ▢

7. Mr. Gomez used 3 boxes of markers in his classroom last week.
   This week he used 2 boxes of markers.

   Unit: ▢

   Group: ▢

8. Abby uses 2 cups of flour in each loaf of bread she makes.

   Unit: ▢

   Group: ▢

9. Laurie saved the same amount of money each week. After 10 weeks she had $80.

   Unit: ▢

   Group: ▢

▶ Write a Definition

10. Write a definition of Multiplication Column Situation and discuss your definition.

▶ Identify Multiplication Column Tables

Decide whether each table is a Multiplication Column Table. Explain why or why not.

11.

0	0
1	9
2	18
3	27
4	36
5	45

12.

0	0
1	4
2	5
3	9
4	10
5	14

13.

0	0
1	11
2	22
3	33
4	44
5	55

14.

0	0
1	3
2	5
3	8
4	10
5	13

15. Write in your Math Journal or tell a different story for each table. Then label each table.

Write your answers on your paper or in your Activity Workbook.

▶ **Linked Multiplication Column Table Situations**

Noreen saves $3 a day. Tim saves $5 a day. They start saving on the same day. The **Linked Multiplication Column Table** and the **Ratio Table** show Noreen's and Tim's savings.

Linked Multiplication Column Table

Days	Noreen ③	Tim ⑤
0	0	0
1	3	5
2	6	10
3	9	15
4	12	20
5	15	25
6	18	30
7	21	35

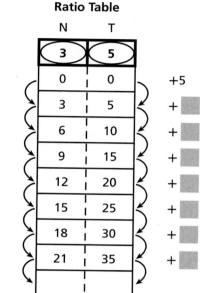

1. How are the tables alike? How are they different?

2. Fill in the numbers at each side of the Ratio Table to show Noreen's and Tim's constant increases.

Use the tables to answer each question.

3. Noreen has saved $12. How much has Tim saved? On which day is this?

4. Tim has saved $35. How much has Noreen saved? On which day is this?

5. On what day will Noreen have $30 in her duck bank? How much will Tim have then?

11-4
Class Activity

Write your answers on your paper or in your Activity Workbook.

▶ Create a Ratio Table

Noreen and Tim bought lots of bags of oranges. Each of Tim's bags cost $6, but Noreen paid only $2 for each bag on sale.

6. Complete the tables for Noreen and Tim. The linking unit is bags of oranges.

Ratio Table

7. How much did 2 bags of oranges cost Noreen? _____ Tim? _____ How much did 4 bags of oranges cost Noreen? _____ Tim? _____

Noreen and Tim plant carrots in their garden. Noreen plants 4 carrot seeds in each row. Tim plants 9 carrot seeds in each row.

8. Fill in the table about Noreen and Tim. The linking unit is _____.

Ratio Table

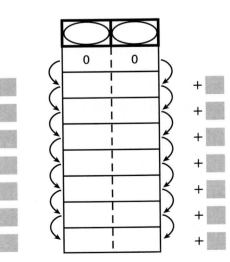

Linked Stories Are Ratios

Write your answers on your paper or in your Activity Workbook.

9. How many carrot seeds will Noreen and Tim each have planted after they have planted 3 rows?
6 rows?
7 rows?

Noreen makes 5 drawings on each page of her sketchbook. Tim makes smaller drawings, so he has 7 drawings on each page of his sketchbook.

10. Fill in the tables. The linking unit is _____.

Linked Multiplication Column Table   **Ratio Table**

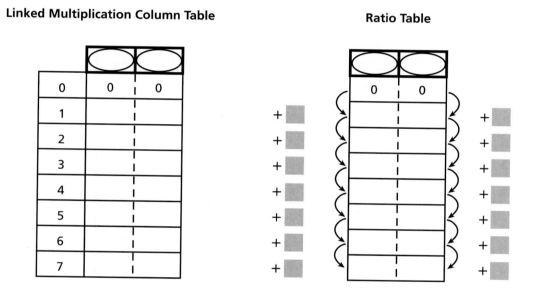

11. What do your tables show about Noreen's and Tim's sketchbooks?

How many drawings do Noreen and Tim each have after they have filled 3 pages?
How many would each have after 5 pages?

How many would each have after 10 pages?

How many would each have after 101 pages?

Class Activity

▶ Recognize Ratio and Non-Ratio Tables

12. Which two tables could be Linked Multiplication Column Tables for Noreen and Tim stories? Why?

A.

⬭	⬭	
0	0	0
1	4	7
2	8	14
3	12	21
4	16	28
5	20	35
6	24	42
7	28	49
8	32	56
9	36	63
10	40	70

B.

⬭	⬭	
0	0	0
1	1	5
2	2	12
3	4	18
4	7	20
5	9	24
6	15	30
7	19	33
8	24	42
9	25	48
10	30	50

C.

⬭	⬭	
0	0	0
1	2	9
2	4	18
3	6	27
4	8	36
5	10	45
6	12	54
7	14	63
8	16	72
9	18	81
10	20	90

D.

⬭	⬭	
0	0	0
1	2	3
2	5	6
3	7	9
4	11	12
5	13	15
6	16	18
7	20	21
8	22	24
9	23	27
10	28	30

13. Why are the other tables not Linked Multiplication Column Tables?

14. Tell a Noreen and Tim story for each of the Linked Multiplication Column Tables above.

Vocabulary

proportion
basic ratio

▶ Proportions and Factor Puzzles

A **proportion** problem comes from a ratio situation. It uses two rows from a Ratio Table. Two multiples of a ratio make a proportion.

A proportion is written in the form

or

$$28 : 12 = 70 : 30$$
$$28 : 12 : : 70 : 30$$

This proportion is read as "28 is to 12 as 70 is to 30."

Here is a proportion problem:
Grandfather bought 14 apples for $6. If I buy the same kind of apples, how much will 35 apples cost?

The problem makes this proportion:

$$14 : 6 = 35 : c$$

To solve the proportion and the problem, you need to find the value of c.

1. Copy and complete the Ratio Table for the problem.

2. Circle the rows of the Ratio Table that make the proportion problem.

   You know how to solve Factor Puzzles. It is faster to make a Factor Puzzle than a whole ratio table.

3. Copy and complete the Factor Puzzle using the numbers in the rows you circled.

4. What is the solution to the apple proportion?

5. You wrote numbers above the Factor Puzzle. Where are they in the ratio table?

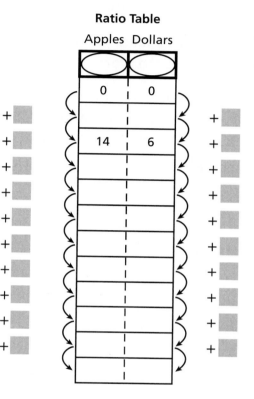

Ratio Table

Apples	Dollars
0	0
14	6

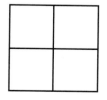

Factor Puzzle

Apples Dollars

This top row of the Ratio Table can be called the **basic ratio**. It is from the _____ row of the multiplication table.

What Are Proportion Situations? **441**

Vocabulary
Factor Puzzle

▶ Solve Proportion Problems

A proportion problem gives you three of the four numbers in a proportion. You can solve a proportion problem by making a Factor Puzzle to show those 2 rows of the Ratio Table.

Use Factor Puzzles to solve these proportion problems about Noreen and Tim.

6. When Noreen planted 6 tomatoes, Tim planted 10 tomatoes. If Noreen plants 21 tomatoes, how many will Tim plant?

N   T

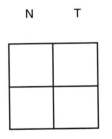

7. When Noreen had 6 stickers, Tim had 21 stickers. How many stickers will Noreen have when Tim has 56?

N   T

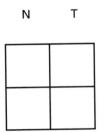

8. Noreen did 72 push-ups while Tim did 32 push-ups. Earlier, while Tim did 12 push-ups, how many did Noreen do?

N   T

9. Noreen saved $20 when Tim saved $35. Later when Noreen saved $24, how much had Tim saved?

N   T

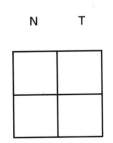

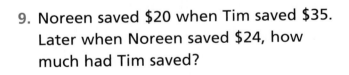

What Are Proportion Situations?

▶ Solve on Your Own

Solve these proportion problems about the twins, Diana and Walter. For each problem, make and solve a Factor Puzzle. For problems 10 and 11, use the basic ratio you find above the Factor Puzzle to make a Ratio Table. Which rows of the Ratio Table make the Factor Puzzle?

10. Diana read 15 pages and Walter read 35. How many pages had Diana read when Walter had read 14?

11. Diana sold 35 tickets and Walter sold 56. How many tickets had Walter sold when Diana had sold 15?

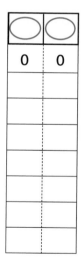

12. Diana sliced 30 bananas while Walter sliced 20. When Diana had sliced 21 bananas, how many had Walter sliced?

▶ Think About Proportions

**Make Factor Puzzles to solve the proportion problems below.
Tell what you assume about each proportion problem. Label
each Factor Puzzle. Circle the unknown number in each puzzle
and use it to answer the question.**

13. Two bands march onto the football field. When Band 1
has 15 people on the field, Band 2 has 6. When Band 2 has
14 people on the field, how many people will Band 1 have?

14. Joshua has 32 angelfish for every 12 snails. When he has
72 angelfish, how many snails will he have?

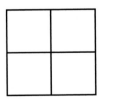

15. Ann planted 25 rose bushes while Ivan planted 30. How many
rose bushes had Ivan planted when Ann had planted 15?

What Are Proportion Situations?

► Solve Problems with Factor Puzzles

Tell which problems are proportion problems, and then solve them with Factor Puzzles. Find the basic ratio in each Factor Puzzle. If a problem is not a proportion problem, tell why.

1. John can plant 7 tomato vines in the time it takes Joanna to plant 4 tomato vines. How many tomato vines will Joanna have planted when John has planted 42 tomato vines?

Show your work on your paper or in your journal.

2. Mr. Tally's class uses 2 bags of markers each week. Ms. Petro's class uses 3 bags of markers one week and 2 the next. If Mr. Tally used 14 bags of markers, how many did Ms. Petro use?

3. In the summer Jason's pond had 14 minnows for each 6 goldfish. Now it has 27 goldfish. How many minnows does it have now?

4. Tom is 12 years old. He is 8 years older than his sister Sylvia. How old were Tom and Sylvia 3 years ago?

▶ Factor Puzzle Multiples in a Ratio Table

Central Middle School has 6 computers and 14 printers.
If East Middle School in the same district has 28 printers,
how many computers does it have?

Here is the Factor Puzzle for this problem.
Use the basic ratio from the top of the
Factor Puzzle to fill in the Ratio Table.

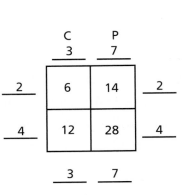

5. How do the numbers 2 and 4, which are at the sides
   of the Factor Puzzle, relate to the Ratio Table?

6. Where are they in the multiplication table?

**Solve the problems below. Make your own Factor Puzzles
if you need them.**

*Show your
work on your paper
or in your journal.*

When there are 6 banana slices in Diana's fruit salad, there
are 14 orange pieces.

7. When there are 28 orange pieces in the fruit salad, how
   many banana slices are there?

8. When there are 56 orange pieces in the fruit salad, how
   many banana slices are there?

9. When there are 18 banana slices in the fruit salad, how
   many orange pieces are there?

Solve Proportion Problems

▶ Solve Numeric Proportion Problems

Solve each proportion by making a Factor Puzzle on another sheet of paper. Then write the basic ratio for each.

1. _____ : 32 = 15 : 40   _____

2. 16 : 36 = _____ : 63   _____

3. 42 : _____ = 54 : 63   _____

4. 14 : 56 = 6 : _____   _____

▶ Identify and Solve Proportion Problems

Tell which are proportion problems. Explain why the others are not. Solve the proportion problems using Factor Puzzles or another method.

5. A bag of 6 oranges costs $2. How many oranges will I get for $10?

6. Cal is 19 and his sister is 13. How old was Cal when his sister was 8?

7. You can make 8 pies from 30 pounds of apples. How many pies can you make from 15 pounds of apples?

8. In the zoo, there are 6 flamingos for every 8 ducks. If there are 20 ducks, how many flamingos are there?

9. Alice is a mail carrier. Today she is delivering letters on Maple Street. She has letters for people living in houses #4 and #6. If she has letters for house #20, what other house do you think she may have letters for?

10. Dana and Sue are sisters. Every week the sisters get an allowance. Dana is older than Sue so she gets more allowance. Now Dana has $48 and Sue has $36. How much will Dana have when Sue has $54?

▶ Match Tables to Problems

11. Which table is not a Ratio Table?

12. Write which story from the previous page is represented by each Ratio Table. One Ratio Table does not represent a story.

13. Which rows in the two story Ratio Tables make up the proportion?

14. Fill in the basic ratio in the blue circles of each Ratio Table.

A.

◯ : ◯
0 : 0
1 : 3
2 : 6
3 : 9
4 : 12
5 : 15
6 : 18
7 : 21

B.

◯ : ◯
0 : 0
6 : 2
12 : 4
18 : 6
24 : 8
30 : 10
36 : 12
42 : 14
48 : 16

C.

◯ : ◯
0 : 0
4 : 3
8 : 6
12 : 9
16 : 12
20 : 15
24 : 18
28 : 21
32 : 24
36 : 27
40 : 30
44 : 33
48 : 36

D.

◯ : ◯
0 : 0
1 : 0
2 : 0
3 : 0
4 : 0
5 : 0
6 : 0
7 : 1
8 : 2
9 : 3
10 : 4
11 : 5
12 : 6
13 : 7
14 : 8
15 : 9
16 : 10
17 : 11
18 : 12
19 : 13
20 : 14

15. On a separate sheet of paper, choose one of your favorite Multiplication Table situations that you wrote on an earlier day and change it to a proportion problem. Make a Ratio Table for your problem.

Solve Proportions as Factor Puzzles

Class Activity

► Use the Basic Ratio

Solve the proportion problems below using Factor Puzzles, and then solve them using a different method.

1. Danny filled each vase with 5 roses and 9 irises. How many irises would he need if he uses 30 roses?

2. $2 : 7 = 10 : y$

► Solve Problems

Tell whether each problem is a proportion problem or not. Tell why you think so, explaining the assumptions you made. Then solve the problem.

3. Martha and Beth walk home from school at different rates. When Martha walks 35 feet, Beth walks 15 feet. How far has Martha walked when Beth has walked 30 feet?

4. If I have 20 blue marbles and 25 red marbles, what is the ratio of blue to red marbles? How many red marbles would be in the same ratio to 8 blue marbles?

5. Maggie bought vegetables at the farmers' market. She chose 6 tomatoes and 9 broccoli bunches. Then she chose 8 carrots. How many heads of lettuce do you think Maggie chose?

6. Every day, Mark and Wanda watch *Nature Journal* together, but Wanda has missed some of the episodes. When Mark had seen 7, Wanda had seen 4. When Mark had seen 10, how many episodes had Wanda seen?

Match three tables with the problems from 3, 4, 5, and 6 that they represent. Which table does not match any problem? Which tables are not Ratio Tables? In the Ratio Tables, which rows make the proportions? Fill in the basic ratios in the blue circles.

A.

◯	◯
0	0
1	0
2	0
3	0
4	1
5	2
6	3
7	4
8	5
9	6
10	7

B.

◯	◯
0	0
5	3
10	4
15	5
20	6
25	7
30	8
35	9
40	10
45	20
50	22

C.

◯	◯
0	0
7	3
14	6
21	9
28	12
35	15
42	18
49	21
56	24
63	27
70	30

D.

◯	◯
0	0
4	5
8	10
12	15
16	20
20	25
24	30
28	35
32	40
36	45
40	50

Basic Ratios

Class Activity

► Write Proportion Problems

Make up a proportion problem for each proportion. Then solve the problem.

Write your word problems on your paper or in your journal.

1. $24 : 36 = 14 : \underline{\hspace{1.5cm}}$

2. $\underline{\hspace{1.5cm}} : 24 = 56 : 32$

► **Practice Solving Proportion Problems**

Show your work on your paper or in your journal.

Decide whether each problem is a proportion problem. Then solve the problem.

3. A turtle crawled 21 meters in 12 minutes. How long did it take her to crawl 14 meters if she crawled at the same rate the whole time?

4. At the Party Store 3 big balloons cost $2. How much will 24 big balloons cost?

5. Every month the public library purchases 10 new fiction books and 7 new DVDs. When the library has purchased 56 new DVDs, how many fiction books will it have purchased?

6. John and Bill drove to Utah for their vacation. They both drove their cars at the same pace, but they left on different days. John left on Day 1 and Bill left 3 days later on Day 4. John got to Utah on Day 6. What day did Bill get to Utah?

7. Mr. Munchkin owns a donut bakery downtown. His donut-making machine is pretty good. Out of every 9 donuts, only 2 are not absolutely perfect. He sells these donuts for less. One day, he baked 54 donuts. How many were not perfect?

8. Two trucks left the dock at exactly the same time and traveled at steady rates. When the first truck had traveled 15 miles, the second truck had traveled 45 miles. How far will the second truck have traveled when the first truck has traveled 30 miles?

Class Activity

Vocabulary

percent

▶ Introduce Percent

1. Use the 100 Pennies page. Circle each **percent** of a set of 100 pennies.

1%	5%	10%	14%
20%	37%	50%	56%
62%	75%	89%	100%

$ 1.00 = 100 pennies

2. Use the percents in exercise 1. Circle each percent on the 100-Millimeter Lines page.

1 decimeter = 10 centimeters
= 100 millimeters

3. Use the percents in exercise 1. Shade each percent on the Small 10 × 10 Grids page.

1 square decimeter
= 100 square centimeters

Class Activity

11-10

▶ Relate Percents, Fractions, and Decimals

For each exercise, show each percent using the 100 Pennies,
100-Millimeter Lines, and the Small 10 × 10 Grids pages.
Write the numerator of each fraction,
and write the equivalent decimals.

4. $10\% = \dfrac{10}{100} = \dfrac{\square}{10}$

   $= 0.10 = 0.1$

5. $20\% = \dfrac{\square}{100} = \dfrac{\square}{10} = \dfrac{\square}{5}$

   $= \square = \square$

6. $30\% = \dfrac{\square}{100} = \dfrac{\square}{10}$

   $= \square = \square$

7. $40\% = \dfrac{\square}{100} = \dfrac{\square}{10} = \dfrac{\square}{5}$

   $= \square = \square$

8. $50\% = \dfrac{\square}{100} = \dfrac{\square}{10} = \dfrac{\square}{2}$

   $= \square = \square$

9. $60\% = \dfrac{\square}{100} = \dfrac{\square}{10} = \dfrac{\square}{5}$

   $= \square = \square$

10. $70\% = \dfrac{\square}{100} = \dfrac{\square}{10}$

    $= \square = \square$

11. $80\% = \dfrac{\square}{100} = \dfrac{\square}{10} = \dfrac{\square}{5}$

    $= \square = \square$

12. $90\% = \dfrac{\square}{100} = \dfrac{\square}{10}$

    $= \square = \square$

13. $100\% = \dfrac{\square}{100} = \dfrac{\square}{10} = \dfrac{\square}{5} = \dfrac{\square}{1}$

    $= \square$

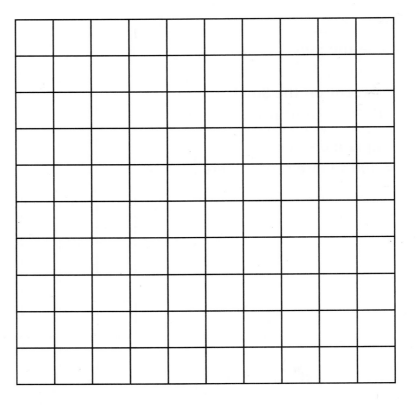

The Meaning of Percent

11-10
Class Activity

14. Discuss patterns you see.

Number line 1 (sixths/thirds):

$\frac{6}{6} = \frac{3}{3}$ | $\frac{5}{6}$ | $\frac{4}{6} = \frac{2}{3}$ | $\frac{3}{6}$ | $\frac{2}{6} = \frac{1}{3}$ | $\frac{1}{6}$ | $\frac{0}{6} = \frac{0}{3}$

Number line 2 (tenths/fifths):

$\frac{10}{10} = \frac{5}{5}$ | $\frac{9}{10}$ | $\frac{8}{10} = \frac{4}{5}$ | $\frac{7}{10}$ | $\frac{6}{10} = \frac{3}{5}$ | $\frac{5}{10}$ | $\frac{4}{10} = \frac{2}{5}$ | $\frac{3}{10}$ | $\frac{2}{10} = \frac{1}{5}$ | $\frac{1}{10}$ | $\frac{0}{10} = \frac{0}{5}$

Number line 3 (eighths/fourths/halves):

$\frac{8}{8} = \frac{4}{4} = \frac{2}{2}$ | $\frac{7}{8}$ | $\frac{6}{8} = \frac{3}{4}$ | $\frac{5}{8}$ | $\frac{4}{8} = \frac{2}{4} = \frac{1}{2}$ | $\frac{3}{8}$ | $\frac{2}{8} = \frac{1}{4}$ | $\frac{1}{8}$ | $\frac{0}{8} = \frac{0}{4} = \frac{0}{2}$

Number line 4 (thousandths):

1.000 | 0.900 | 0.800 | 0.700 | 0.600 | 0.500 | 0.400 | 0.300 | 0.200 | 0.100 | 0.000

Number line 5 (hundredths):

1.00 | 0.90 | 0.80 | 0.70 | 0.60 | 0.50 | 0.40 | 0.30 | 0.20 | 0.10 | 0.00

Number line 6 (tenths):

1.0 | 0.9 | 0.8 | 0.7 | 0.6 | 0.5 | 0.4 | 0.3 | 0.2 | 0.1 | 0.0

Number line 7 (percent):

100% | 90% | 80% | 75% | 70% | 60% | 50% | 40% | 30% | 25% | 20% | 10% | 0%

▶ Practice Percent Equivalencies

15. Fill in the missing percents, decimals, and fractions.

Your teacher will give you a copy of this page.

		Percent, Decimal, and Fraction Equivalencies			
Cents	Percent of a dollar	Dollars	Decimal	Fraction of 100	Simplest fraction
40 ¢	40%	$0.40	0.40	$\frac{40}{100}$	$\frac{2}{5}$
75 ¢					
	25%				
			0.50		
			0.60		
				$\frac{30}{100}$	
					$\frac{4}{5}$
		$1.00			
		$0.10			
					$\frac{9}{10}$
				$\frac{20}{100}$	
	70%				

Make your drawings on a separate sheet of paper.

► Solve Percent Problems with Diagrams

Solve the problems. Use what you know about fractions and percents.

This is 20% of a figure.

1. Draw 80% of the figure.

2. Draw 100% of the figure.

3. Draw 120% of the figure.

4. Draw 200% of the figure.

This is 25% of a figure.

5. Draw 100% of the figure.

6. Draw 150% of the figure.

Make your drawings on a separate sheet of paper.

This is 75% of a figure.

7. Draw 100% of the figure.

8. Draw 25% of the figure.

Here is 75% of a design.

9. Draw 100% of the design.

10. Draw 150% of the design.

11. This is 150% of a figure.

Draw 100% of the figure.

This is 200% of a figure.

12. Draw the figure.

13. Draw 150% of the figure.

Solve Problems Using Percents

► Solve Numeric Percent Problems

14. What is 25% of 32?

	Percent	Number
Part	25	☐
Whole	100	32

$$\frac{25}{100} = \frac{\square}{32}$$

Why do we write $\frac{25}{100}$?

Why is 32 in the denominator?

Solve by simplifying: $\frac{25}{100} = \frac{\square}{\square} = \frac{\square}{32}$

15. 27 is 30% of what?

	Percent	Number
Part	30	27
Whole	100	☐

$$\frac{30}{100} = \frac{27}{\square}$$

Why do we write $\frac{30}{100}$?

Why is 27 in the numerator?

Solve by simplifying: $\frac{30}{100} = \frac{\square}{\square} = \frac{27}{\square}$

16. 21 is what percent of 28?

	Percent	Number
Part	☐	21
Whole	100	28

$$\frac{\square}{100} = \frac{21}{28}$$

Why is the unknown number above 100?

Why is 21 above 28?

Solve by simplifying: $\frac{21}{28} = \frac{\square}{\square} = \square$

17. What is 125% of 28?

	Percent	Number
Part	125	☐
Whole	100	28

$$\frac{125}{100} = \frac{\square}{28}$$

Why is the part greater than the whole?

Why is 28 in the denominator?

Will the unknown number be greater than or less than 28? Why?

Solve by simplifying: $\frac{125}{100} = \frac{\square}{\square} = \frac{\square}{28}$

Set up a proportion and solve by simplifying and finding an equivalent fraction.

18. 75% of 24 is _____.

19. 28 is 80% of _____.

20. What percent of 36 is 9? _____

21. 140% of 30 is _____.

▶ Solve Word Problems

Solve the word problems using any method.

22. In Mr. Roberts's class there are 30 children. 18 of them are girls. What percent of the children in Mr. Roberts's class are girls?

23. Andrew counted 20 fish in the pond at City Park. 15 were goldfish and the rest were carp. What percent of the fish were goldfish?

24. A jug holds 80 mL of water when it is full. How much water will there be in the jug when it is 75% full?

25. After a long diet, the dog Lucky weighed 54 pounds. That was 90% of his old weight. How much did Lucky weigh before the diet?

26. Emma saw a movie 4 times. That is only 80% of the number of times Yoko has seen it. How many times has Yoko seen the movie?

27. Kevin made 55 sandwiches for the party. 33 of the sandwiches were tuna. What percent of the sandwiches were tuna?

28. Chip has already eaten 320 of the 400 acorns he collected for winter. What percent of his acorns has Chip eaten?

29. In Mr. Smith's front yard there is an olive tree and a palm tree. The olive tree is 12 feet tall and the palm tree is 15 feet tall. The olive tree's height is what percent of the palm tree's height?

▶ Solve Probability Problems

Solve each problem using any method.

1. A box of 40 crayons has 10 shades of red, 6 shades of blue, 4 shades of yellow, 2 shades of purple, as well as other colors. What is the probability of getting a red crayon? A blue crayon? A yellow crayon? A purple crayon? Express your answers as a percent.

2. The grab bag at the town picnic contained 2,000 tickets to local baseball games. 40% were Pigeon tickets, 35% were Robin tickets, and 25% were Sparrow tickets. If you drew out 20 tickets, how many tickets for each team would you expect to get? How many Pigeon tickets are there?

3. Peppy the cat sleeps 18 hours a day. What is the percent chance that you will find Peppy asleep at any one time of day?

4. A bushel of apples contains 32 Jonathan apples, 28 Golden Delicious apples, and 20 Granny Smith apples. What are your chances of picking one Jonathan apple from the bushel? Express your answer as a percent.

5. What are your chances of each spinner landing on a dark space? Express your answers as a percent.

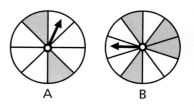

A   B

6. Of the 5,000 children who live in Garden Town, 4,500 love to eat vegetables.

   What percent of the children love to eat vegetables?

7. Of the 30 children who live on Green Bean Street in Garden Town, how many probably do not like to eat vegetables?

8. A basket of 30 vegetables has 12 carrots, 6 tomatoes, 3 heads of lettuce, and 9 mushrooms. What is the probability of picking a carrot? A tomato? A head of lettuce? A mushroom? Express your answers as percents.

9. Dorothy bought a bag of 500 mixed flower seeds. The bag contained 250 dahlia seeds, 120 daisy seeds, 75 violet seeds, and the rest were forget-me-nots. Dorothy planted 200 of the seeds in her garden. How many of each flower can she expect to grow in her garden?

Vocabulary

similar
ratio

▶ Discuss Similar Figures

When figures are similar, the measures of corresponding angles are equal and the lengths of corresponding sides are proportional: they share the same ratio.

All of these rectangles are similar.

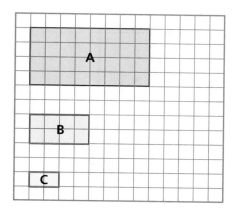

Two of these triangles are similar.

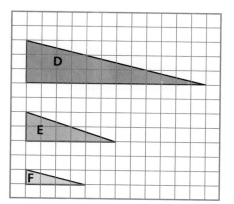

1. Write a ratio $b : h$ that compares the lengths of the base and the height.

   A _____ B _____ C _____

2. Write a ratio $b : h$ that compares the lengths of the base and the height. Which triangles are similar?

   D _____ E _____ F _____

Is each pair of figures similar? Write *yes* or *no*. Show why or why not with ratios.

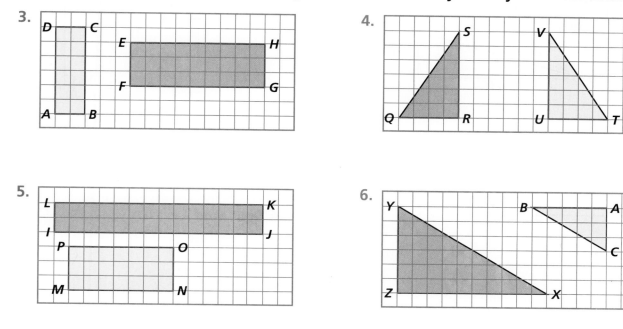

▶ Rotating or Reflecting

Sometimes you need to rotate or reflect similar figures to find the corresponding sides to make ratios.

Write the ratios from these similar figures in a Factor Puzzle to find each unknown side.

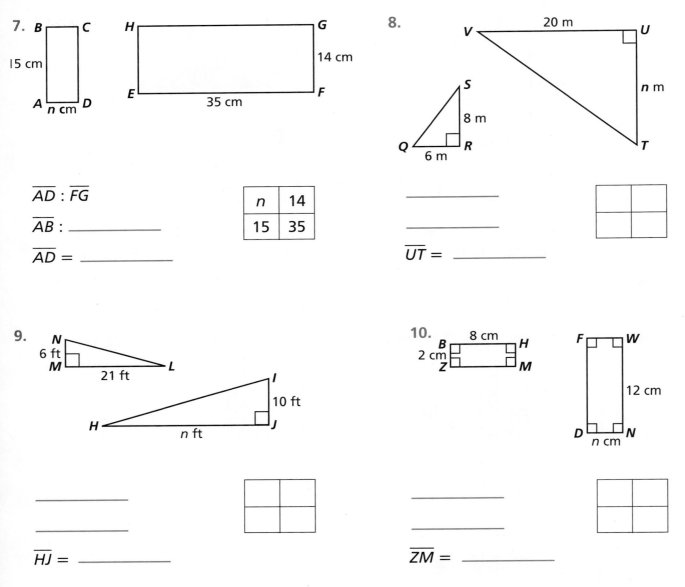

7.

$\overline{AD} : \overline{FG}$

$\overline{AB}$: _____

$\overline{AD} =$ _____

n	14
15	35

8.

_____

_____

$\overline{UT} =$ _____

9.

_____

_____

$\overline{HJ} =$ _____

10.

_____

_____

$\overline{ZM} =$ _____

▶ Similar Triangles

Anna and Fumi want to know how tall the school flagpole is. They have a stick that is 8 feet long. Discuss these questions about how they can use the stick and shadows to answer their question.

- What is true about the lengths of the objects and their shadows?

- Does it matter how high the sun is in the sky?

- If the shadow of the flagpole is 7 ft long and the shadow of the stick is 2 ft long, how tall is the flagpole?

Solve. Use what you know about similar triangles.

11. Two students measure their shadows on a sunny day. The student who is 63 in. tall has a shadow of 35 in. How tall is the student whose shadow is 30 in. long?

12. Joshua and Erin measure the shadows made by their houses. Joshua's house has a 30-foot shadow and Erin's has a 35-foot shadow. Erin knows that her house is 21 ft tall. How tall is Joshua's house?

13. The shorter statue in the park has a height of 12 feet and a shadow of 15 feet. The shadow of the taller statue is 30 feet long. What is the height of the taller statue?

14. Two buildings have shadows that are the same length. What is true about their heights?

15. Martha's height is 5 ft, 2 inches. She is twice as tall as her 2-year-old sister. Her sister's shadow is 3 feet long. How long is Martha's shadow?

11–13
Going Further

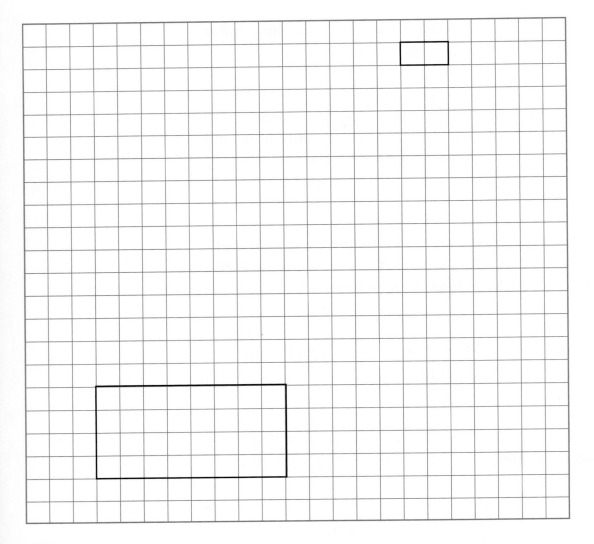

> Write your answers on your paper or in your Activity Workbook.

▶ Show Perspective

Similarity can be used to show perspective. The smaller a figure is, the farther away it appears. The small rectangle represents a rectangle that is the same size as the big rectangle. It is just farther away.

1. To show perspective, use your ruler to draw lines to connect corresponding vertices on the similar rectangles.

2. Find other rectangles that fit within the lines you drew. Put their bases and heights in the table. Some may have fractional bases and heights.

b : h
8 : 4
2 : 1

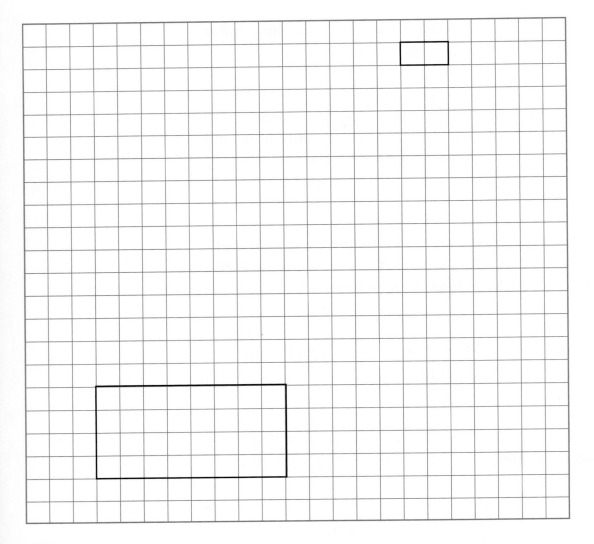

Similar Figures

Dear Family,

In this unit, your child is introduced to similarity and scale. There are two main goals for this topic:

1. Students will identify and draw similar figures, and they will use similarity to find a missing measurement.

   - One figure is similar to another if it has the same shape. It may be enlarged or reduced.

   - In similar figures, the measurements of corresponding angles are equal and corresponding side lengths share the same ratio.

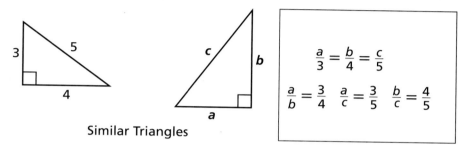

Similar Triangles

$$\frac{a}{3} = \frac{b}{4} = \frac{c}{5}$$

$$\frac{a}{b} = \frac{3}{4} \quad \frac{a}{c} = \frac{3}{5} \quad \frac{b}{c} = \frac{4}{5}$$

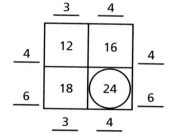

A Factor Puzzle can be used to find an unknown length in a similarity problem.

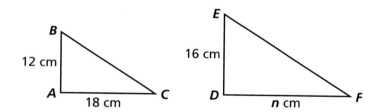

For these similar triangles, students can make and solve the Factor Puzzle shown in the margin to find that the unknown length is 24 cm.

2. Students will analyze and interpret scale drawings, including maps, and make two-dimensional scale drawings.

   - In scale drawings and maps, the actual object and the drawing are similar.

   - The scale tells the relationship between the distances on the drawing or map and the actual distances. For example, $\frac{1}{4}$ inch = 100 miles means that every $\frac{1}{4}$ inch on the map represents 100 actual miles.

If you have any questions or comments, please call or write to me.

Sincerely,
Your child's teacher

Your teacher will give you a copy of this letter.

Estimada familia:

En esta unidad su niño empieza a estudiar la semejanza y las escalas. Este tema tiene dos objetivos principales:

1. Los estudiantes identificarán y dibujarán figuras semejantes y usarán la semejanza para hallar una medida que falta.

   • Una figura es semejante a otra si tiene la misma forma. El tamaño de la figura puede aumentar o disminuir.

   • En figuras semejantes, las medidas de los ángulos correspondientes son iguales y las longitudes de los lados correspondientes tienen la misma razón.

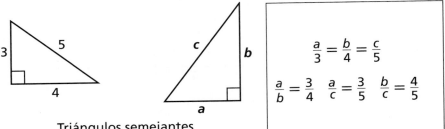

Triángulos semejantes

$$\frac{a}{3} = \frac{b}{4} = \frac{c}{5}$$

$$\frac{a}{b} = \frac{3}{4} \qquad \frac{a}{c} = \frac{3}{5} \qquad \frac{b}{c} = \frac{4}{5}$$

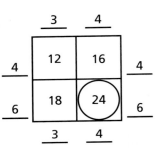

Se puede usar un rompecabezas de factores para hallar una longitud desconocida en un problema de semejanza.

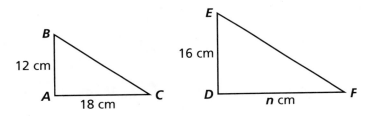

Para estos triángulos semejantes, los estudiantes pueden hacer y resolver el rompecabezas de factores que se muestra en el margen y determinar que la longitud desconocida es 24 cm.

2. Los estudiantes analizarán e interpretarán dibujos a escala, incluyendo mapas, y harán dibujos bidimensionales a escala.

   • En los dibujos a escala y en los mapas, el objeto real y el dibujo son semejantes.

   • La escala indica la relación entre las distancias en el dibujo o mapa y las distancias reales. Por ejemplo: $\frac{1}{4}$ de pulgada = 100 millas significa que cada $\frac{1}{4}$ de pulgada del mapa representa 100 millas reales.

Si tiene alguna duda o comentario, por favor comuníquese conmigo.

Atentamente,
El maestro de su niño

Tu maestro te dará una copia de esta carta.

Similar Figures

► Read a Map

A map is an example of a **scale drawing**. On the map below, every inch represents a specified distance. To find the distance that an inch represents, use the **scale** located on the map.

1. What distance does each inch on the map represent?

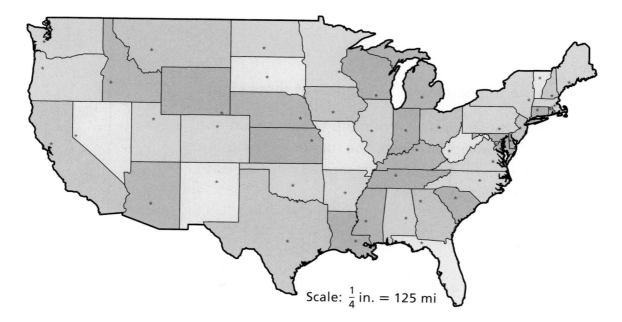

Scale: $\frac{1}{4}$ in. = 125 mi

Use the map and an inch ruler to answer each question below.

2. Choose a state capital and write its name.

3. Locate another state capital and write its name.

4. To the nearest fifty miles, what is the distance between the capitals?

▶ Plan a Trip

Use the map on the previous page and an inch ruler to answer the questions below.

5. List four states you might like to visit someday.

6. On the map, write the names of the capitals of those states.

7. Plan a trip to visit those capitals. Your trip should begin and end at your own state capital. Write the names of the capitals in the order you will visit them. Which capital will you visit first? Which will you visit second?

8. Using the map scale and an inch ruler, estimate the total distance you will travel, to the nearest hundred miles.

9. If you change the order in which you visit the capitals, will the total distance of your trip change? Explain.

10. In which order should you visit the capitals so that your trip is the shortest possible distance? What is that distance?

▶ Will It Fit?

Vocabulary

scale drawing

In a **scale drawing**, the scale tells how the measurements in the drawing relate to the actual measurements.

Use a centimeter ruler to measure the rugs in exercises 1 and 2. Then decide if each rug will fit in your classroom. Write *yes* or *no*.

1. To the right is a view of a rug drawn to the scale
   1 cm = 60 cm.

1 cm = 60 cm

2. This is a view of a different rug drawn to the scale 1 cm = 2 m.

1 cm = 2 m

3. If the scale in exercise 2 were changed to 1 cm = 1 m, how would the size of the actual rug change? Explain your answer.

Class Activity

Your teacher will give you a copy of Quarter-Inch Grid Paper.

▶ Draw to Scale

Choose an object in your classroom with a rectangular shape, such as your desktop or a window. Use Quarter-Inch Grid Paper to make a scale drawing of the object. Include the scale.

Explore Scale Drawings

Write your answers on your paper or in your Activity Workbook.

Vocabulary

floor plan

▶ Discuss a Floor Plan

When interior designers draw a **floor plan** of a room, they often suggest where furniture should be placed. The floor plan below is a scale drawing of a room.

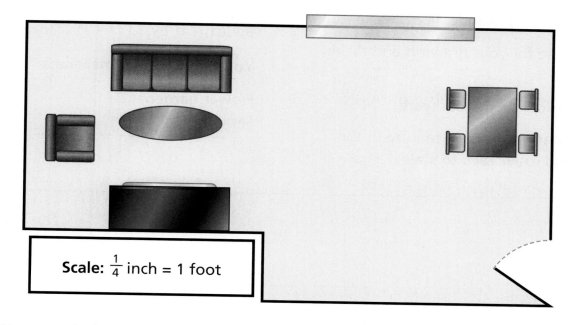

Scale: $\frac{1}{4}$ inch = 1 foot

Use your inch ruler and the scale to answer each question below.

1. What is the length of the actual sofa?

2. What is the length of the actual armchair?

3. How much floor space does the actual dining room table take up?

4. About how far from the actual sofa is the TV?

5. How wide is the actual window?

6. Explain why you cannot determine the height of the window.

7. Draw a bookshelf in the room. What is the width and the depth of the bookshelf you drew? What is its actual width and actual depth?

Your teacher will give you a copy of Quarter-Inch Grid Paper.

▶ Make a Scale Drawing

The table on the right describes a backyard and its features.

On Quarter-Inch Grid Paper, make a scale drawing of the backyard and include all of the features.

- Choose a scale for your drawing and make a key.

- Draw the border of the backyard.

- Choose a location for each feature in the backyard and draw each to scale.

Actual Dimensions

Yard: 400 sq ft
Patio: 10 ft by 12 ft
Picnic table: 4 ft by 6 ft
Children's pool: 4 ft in diameter
Bench: 1 ft by 3 ft

You Choose the Dimensions

Flower garden:
Sandbox:

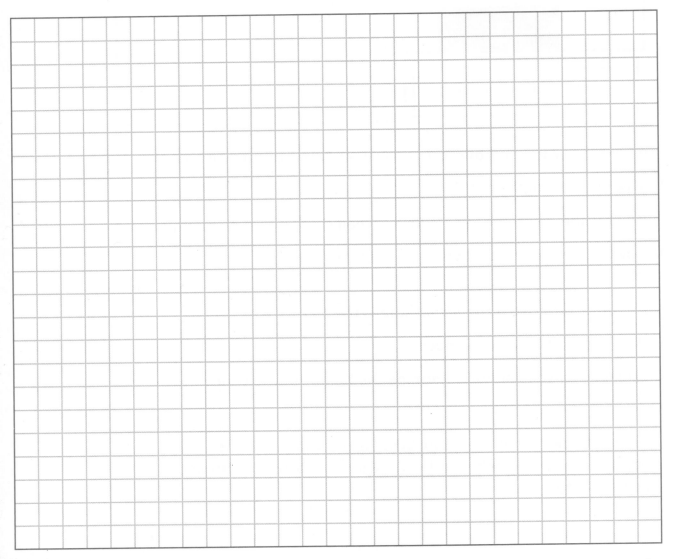

Use Scale Drawings

▶ Math and Advertising

The nutrition magazine at the right, like many magazines, depends on advertising in order to stay in business. One half of the total layout is for advertising. Look at the layout for the magazine page.

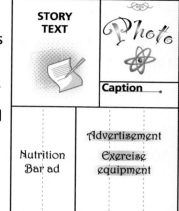

Magazine Layout Page

1. Two-fifths of the page will be covered by a photo of the food pyramid. What percent is that?

2. The designer marked the space for the caption 0.05. What percent of the page will the caption cover?

3. What fraction of this page is marked for the story? Write the part as a percent.

4. Which ad takes up the greatest percent of space on the page? Write the percent.

5. What percent of the page is reserved for the smaller ad?

6. What percent of the total layout is for advertising?

7. List the contents of each part of this page layout and write the percent of the page it represents. What is the sum of the percents?

8. Design a magazine page of your own. Draw a sketch on a separate sheet of paper. Write what you would put in each section and the percent of the page it would be. Find the total of the percents.

▶ Sweet Scents

Mavis has a candle and soap-making business. She wants to know the most popular scent, so she can use it in her products.

9. What might her hypothesis be?

10. What survey question could she ask to test the hypothesis? Who should she survey? How many people should she ask?

11. How might she use observation to test the hypothesis?

12. What differences can you expect in the results by observation and the results by survey?

13. Design a short investigation that you can do within your classroom. Collect data using a survey and by observation.

- My hypothesis is

- My observation method is

- My survey question is

14. How did the data collection method affect the results?

Use Mathematical Processes

1. Make a Ratio Table for this situation. Be sure to label your table.

   A fruit salad recipe calls for 7 bananas for every 3 oranges.

2. Grandma Jackson has 35 tomato plants in 7 equal rows of her garden. Complete this statement.

   Grandma Jackson has

   _____ per _____.

Ratio Table

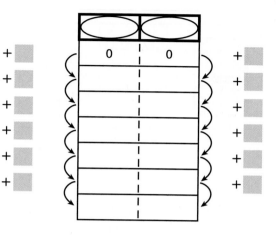

Solve each problem.

3. Janet drives 10 miles in 16 minutes. How long does it take her to drive 45 miles at the same rate?

Show your work on your paper or in your journal.

4. Al had $75 when he went shopping. He spent 60% of his money. How much money did he have left when he came home?

5. A bag of 25 marbles contains 8 red marbles. If one marble is picked from the bag, what is the probability that it is red? Express your answer as a percent.

Is each pair of figures similar? Write *yes* or *no*.

6.

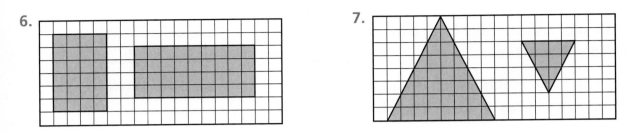

7.

8. This scale drawing shows that the distance from Orrville to Beetown is 60 km. What is the distance from Orrville to King City?

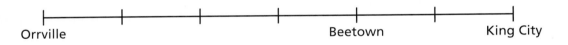

Orrville   Beetown   King City

9. The two figures are similar. Find the unknown measurement.

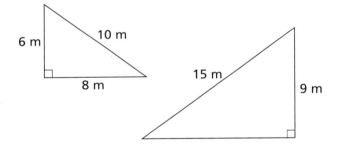

6 m   10 m

8 m

15 m   9 m

10. **Extended Response** Write a word problem for the proportion, and show how to solve the problem.

$$n : 35 = 18 : 42$$

Class Activity

Vocabulary

rectangular prism
face
base

▶ Make a Rectangular Prism from a Net

1. The sides of a **rectangular prism** are called **faces**. How many faces does a rectangular prism have?

2. The top and bottom of a rectangular prism are called **bases**. What shape are the bases of a rectangular prism?

3. What shape are the other faces?

Use the rectangular prism at the right for questions 4–5.

4. What are the dimensions of the bases of this rectangular prism?

5. What are the dimensions of the other faces?

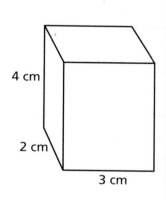

4 cm

2 cm

3 cm

6. Measure and record the dimensions of the prism you made.

Class Activity

▶ **Draw a Net for a Rectangular Prism**

Draw a net for a rectangular prism with dimensions 2 cm by 3 cm by 4 cm as shown on page 479. Think about how the faces will be connected to the bases and to each other. Consider how you will position the faces so the net will fit on the centimeter grid.

Make your drawings on grid paper or in your Activity Workbook.

Prisms and Cylinders

12–1 Class Activity

Vocabulary

base
prism

▶ Identify Prisms

Write the shape of the base and use it to name the prism.

7.

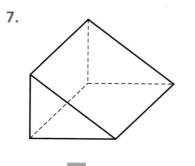

Base: ⬜

Name: ⬜

8.

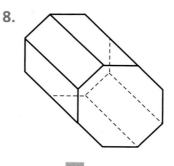

Base: ⬜

Name: ⬜

9.

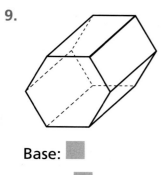

Base: ⬜

Name: ⬜

10.

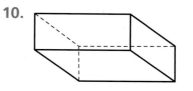

Base: ⬜

Name: ⬜

11.

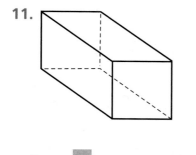

Base: ⬜

Name: ⬜

12.

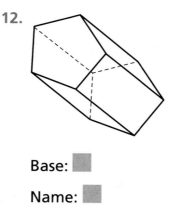

Base: ⬜

Name: ⬜

Vocabulary

cylinder
net
circumference

▶ **Discuss Cylinders**

These are examples of a special kind of solid called a **cylinder**.

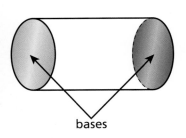

bases

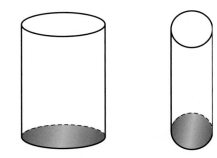

13. List three real-world examples of cylinders.

14. How is a cylinder like a prism?

15. How is a cylinder different from a prism?

▶ **Nets for Cylinders**

16. Explain how to make a cylinder from this **net**.

17. How is the length of the rectangle related to the **circumference** of each circle?

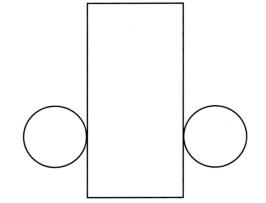

► Match Nets and Solids

Match each net in the first column to a solid in the second column. The nets are smaller than the solids.

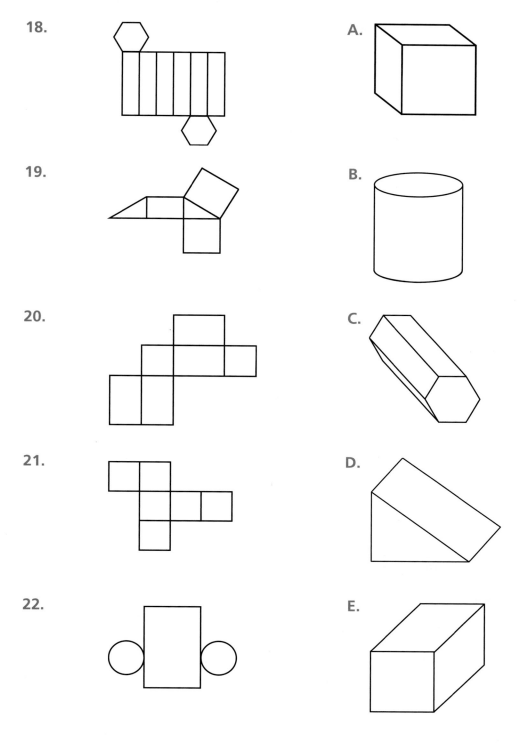

18.

19.

20.

21.

22.

A.

B.

C.

D.

E.

▶ Find Surface Area

These nets form prisms. Find the missing dimensions. Then find the surface area of each prism.

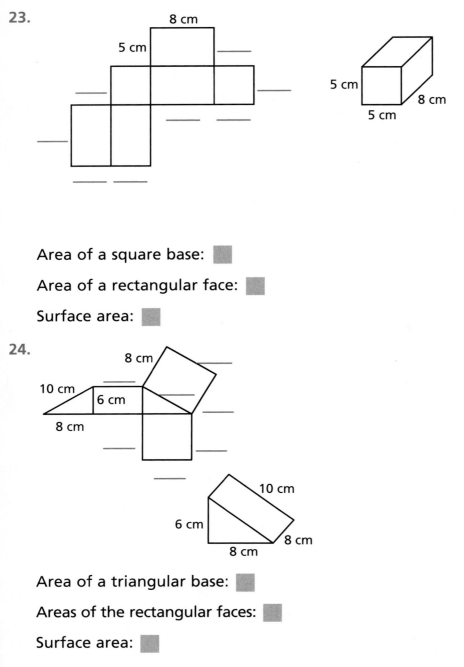

23.

8 cm

5 cm

5 cm

5 cm 8 cm

5 cm

Area of a square base: ▨

Area of a rectangular face: ▨

Surface area: ▨

24.

8 cm

10 cm

6 cm

8 cm

10 cm

6 cm

8 cm

8 cm

Area of a triangular base: ▨

Areas of the rectangular faces: ▨

Surface area: ▨

25. How can you find the surface area of any prism?

Name each prism and find its surface area.

Vocabulary

edge
cube
face

26.

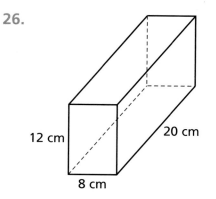

12 cm 20 cm

8 cm

Show your work on your paper or in your journal.

27.

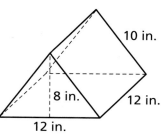

10 in.

8 in. 12 in.

12 in.

The edges of this cube are 3 cm long.

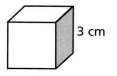

3 cm

28. What is the area of each **face**?

29. What is the surface area of the cube?

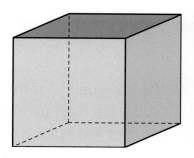

30. Write one sentence that describes how to find the surface area of a cube.

▶ Solve Problems About Surface Area and Volume

A cube has a surface area of 24 square meters.

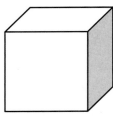

31. What is the area of each face?

32. What is the length of each edge?

Surface area = 24 sq m

The surface area of a cube is 54 square centimeters.

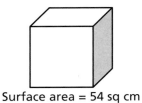

33. What is the area of each face of the cube?

34. What is the length of each edge?

Surface area = 54 sq cm

One face of a cube has an area of 16 square millimeters.

35. What is the surface area of the cube?

Area of one face = 16 sq mm

36. What is the length of each edge?

37. What is the volume of the cube?

A cube has a volume of 8 cubic decimeters.

38. What is the length of each edge?

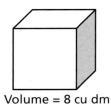

39. What is the area of each face?

Volume = 8 cu dm

40. Pedro glued together 8 one-inch cubes to make a bigger cube. He then painted the cube red. In square inches, what area of the cube is covered by red paint?

Dear Family,

In this unit, we are studying three-dimensional or solid figures. Your child will learn the properties of three-dimensional figures and will be able to describe, compare, and draw conclusions about figures from the number of faces, edges, and vertices. These three-dimensional figures include prisms, cylinders, pyramids, and cones, as shown below.

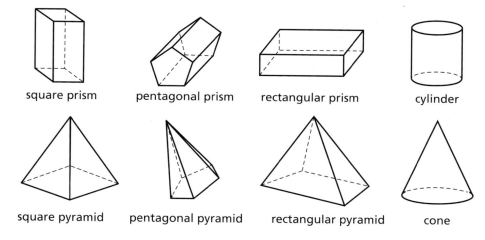

square prism   pentagonal prism   rectangular prism   cylinder

square pyramid   pentagonal pyramid   rectangular pyramid   cone

You can become an active part of your child's learning by asking questions about these figures. For example, you might point to a figure and ask:

- What is the name of this figure?

- What is the shape of its base?

- How many bases does it have?

- How many faces does it have?

- What is the shape of each face?

Your teacher will give you a copy of this letter.

Your child will also explore rotational symmetry of three-dimensional figures. A figure has *rotational symmetry* if it can be rotated less than 360° around its center point and still look exactly the same as the original figure.

If you need practice materials or if you have any questions, please call or write to me.

Sincerely,
Your child's teacher

Estimada familia:

En esta unidad estamos estudiando figuras tridimensionales o cuerpos geométricos. Su hijo/a aprenderá las propiedades de las figuras tridimensionales y podrá describir, comparar y sacar conclusiones sobre estas figuras de acuerdo con el número de caras, aristas y vértices. Entre las figuras tridimensionales se encuentran los prismas, cilindros, pirámides y conos, tal como se muestran a continuación.

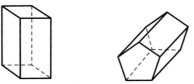 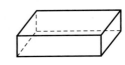

prisma cuadrangular   prisma pentagonal   prisma rectangular   cilindro

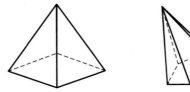 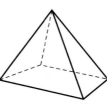 

pirámide cuadrangular   pirámide pentagonal   pirámide rectangular   cono

Ud. puede convertirse en parte activa en el proceso de aprendizaje de su hijo/a pidiéndole que responda a las siguientes preguntas sobre estas figuras. Por ejemplo, Ud. podría señalar una de las figuras y preguntar:

- ¿Cómo se llama esta figura?
- ¿Qué forma tiene la base?
- ¿Cuántas bases tiene?
- ¿Cuántas caras tiene?
- ¿Qué forma tiene cada cara?

Su hijo/a también explorará la simetría rotacional de figuras tridimensionales. Una figura tiene *simetría rotacional,* si al rotarla menos de 360° alrededor de su punto central, todavía coincide exactamente con la figura original.

Si Ud. necesita materiales de práctica o si tiene alguna pregunta, por favor comuníquese conmigo.

Atentamente,
El maestro de su niño

Tu maestro te dará una copia de esta carta.

Vocabulary

pyramid

► **Compare Pyramids**

Pyramids have been used in architecture for many centuries.

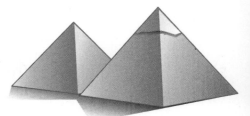

About 4,000 years ago, Egyptians built huge pyramids of stone blocks. These illustrations show two of the three famous pyramids of Giza. They still stand along the Nile River near the city of Cairo.

About 2,000 years ago, the Mayan people built step pyramids to help them track the seasons of the year. This illustration shows the step pyramid in Chichen Itza, Mexico.

In 1983, Chinese American architect I.M. Pei was invited to design a glass pyramid for the famous Louvre Museum in Paris, France. This pyramid serves as a skylight for the main entrance to the museum, which is one floor below the pyramid.

A pyramid, like a prism, can have any polygon for a base.

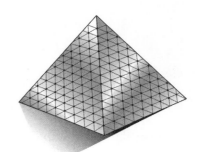

1. What makes pyramids A and B like each other?

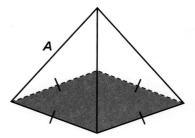

2. What makes them different?

3. Write a different name for each pyramid.

    A

    B

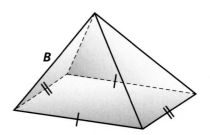

4. How is a cone similar to a pyramid?

5. How is a cone different from a pyramid?

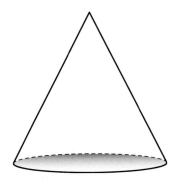

► **Discuss Pyramids**

Name the shape of the base and use it to name the pyramid.

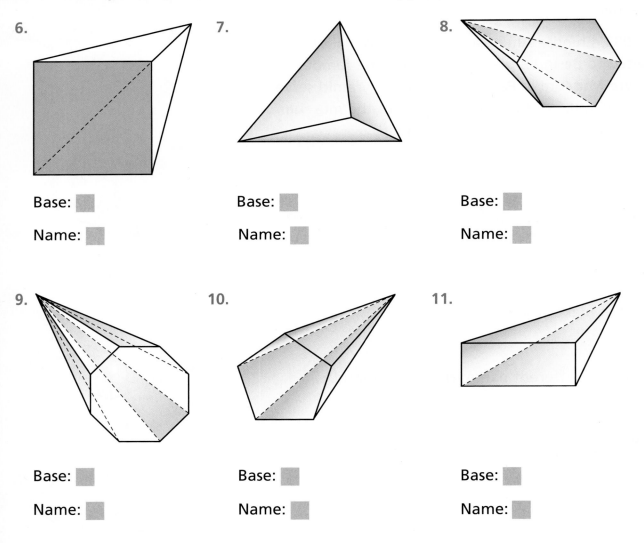

6.

Base: ▢

Name: ▢

7.

Base: ▢

Name: ▢

8.

Base: ▢

Name: ▢

9.

Base: ▢

Name: ▢

10.

Base: ▢

Name: ▢

11.

Base: ▢

Name: ▢

► Pyramids and Nets

Match each net to a solid. The nets do not match the solids exactly.

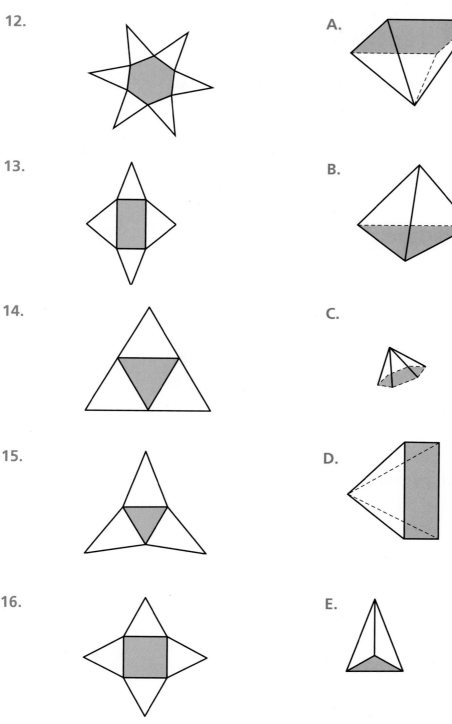

12.

A.

13.

B.

14.

C.

15.

D.

16.

E.

▶ Find Surface Area

These nets form pyramids. Find the surface area of each net.

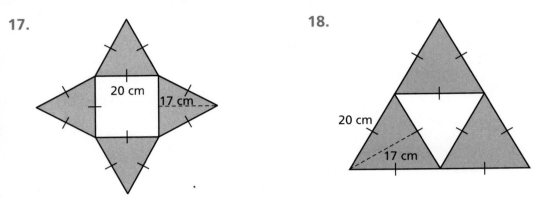

17.

20 cm

17 cm

18.

20 cm

17 cm

19.

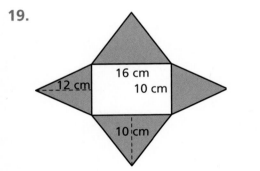

16 cm

10 cm

12 cm

10 cm

20.

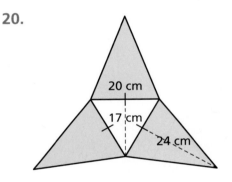

20 cm

17 cm

24 cm

Find the surface area of each pyramid.

21.

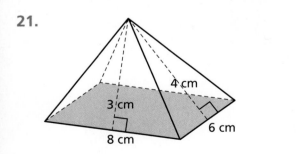

4 cm

3 cm

6 cm

8 cm

22.

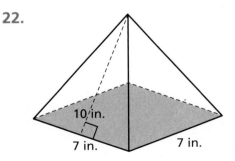

10 in.

7 in.

7 in.

▶ Draw Two-Dimensional Views

These **views** show what a solid figure looks like from the front, side, and top.

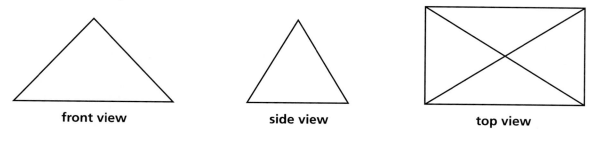

1. Which solid matches the views shown above?

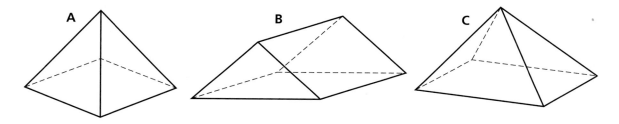

Draw the front, side, and top views of the other two solids.
Then name each solid.

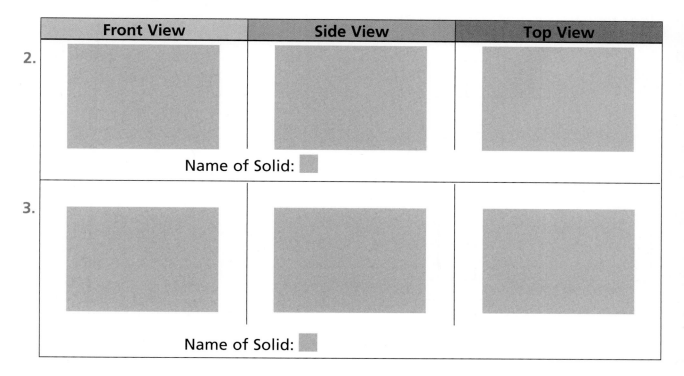

	Front View	Side View	Top View
2.			
	Name of Solid:		
3.			
	Name of Solid:		

▶ Draw Pictures of Solids

Below are three different views of the figure at the right.

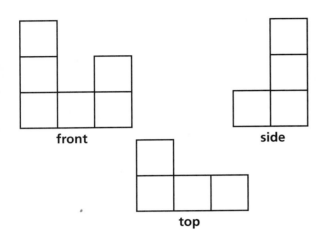

front

side

top

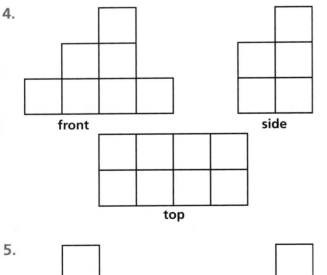

side

front

Make a drawing on Triangle-Grid Paper to match the views.

4.

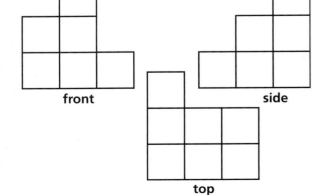

front

side

top

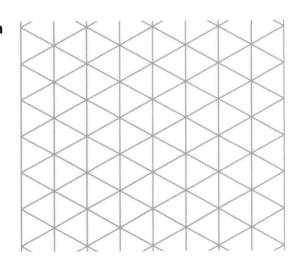

5.

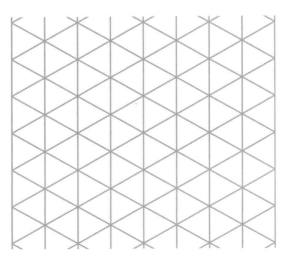

front

side

top

Compare and Contrast Geometric Solids

► Compare and Contrast Faces, Edges, and Vertices

Complete the table.

Figure	Number of Sides of a Base	Number of Faces	Number of Edges	Number of Vertices
Triangular Prism				
Triangular Pyramid				
Square Prism				
Square Pyramid				
Pentagonal Prism				
Pentagonal Pyramid				
Hexagonal Prism				
Hexagonal Pyramid				

▶ Draw Conclusions About Prisms and Pyramids

6. What shape are all of the faces of a pyramid, except the base?

7. How does the number of faces a pyramid has compare to the number of sides its base has?

8. The number of vertices a prism has is how many times the number of sides its base has?

9. A pyramid has 12 edges. How many vertices does a prism with the same base have?

10. A prism has 10 faces. How many faces does a pyramid with the same base have?

11. What other conclusions can you draw about prisms and pyramids?

Compare and Contrast Geometric Solids

▶ Rotating Cubes

The number cubes for exercises 1–8 are the same as your paper number cube models. The red lines show the **axes of rotation.**

Orient the cube so 2 is facing you. The axis of rotation is through the center of the 1 and 6 faces of the cube. What number is on the front after each rotation?

1. $\frac{1}{4}$ rotation **clockwise**

2. $\frac{1}{4}$ rotation **counterclockwise**

3. $\frac{1}{2}$ rotation

4. $\frac{3}{4}$ rotation clockwise

Orient the cube so 2 is facing you. The axis of rotation is through the center of the 2 and 5 faces of the cube. What number is on top after each rotation?

5. $\frac{1}{4}$ rotation clockwise

6. $\frac{1}{4}$ rotation counterclockwise

7. $\frac{1}{2}$ rotation

8. $\frac{3}{4}$ rotation clockwise

Orient the cube so 4 is facing you. The axis of rotation is through the center of the 3 and 4 faces of the cube. What number is on top after each rotation?

9. $\frac{1}{4}$ rotation clockwise

10. $\frac{1}{2}$ rotation

12–4

Class Activity

Vocabulary

rotational symmetry

▶ Rotational Symmetry

These solid figures have **rotational symmetry**. They look identical after less than one complete 360° rotation. The red lines show the axes of rotation.

Looks the Same After			
every $\frac{1}{2}$ of a complete rotation	every $\frac{1}{4}$ of a complete rotation	every $\frac{1}{3}$ of a complete rotation	every $\frac{1}{6}$ of a complete rotation
prism with non-square rectangles for all 6 faces	pyramid with a square base	prism with equilateral triangles for top and bottom bases	prism with regular hexagons for top and bottom bases

After what fraction of a rotation does each figure look the same?

11. prism with square base

12. pyramid with rectangular base

13. This shape has isosceles triangles for bases. Explain why it does not have rotational symmetry for the red axis of rotation.

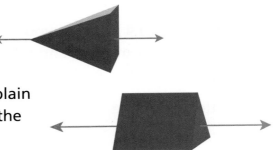

Name the solid. Describe its rotational symmetry.

1.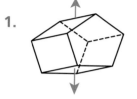

2.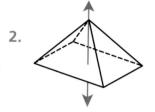

3.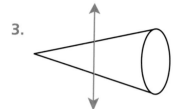

4.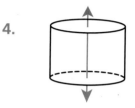

Find the surface area of each three-dimensional figure.

5.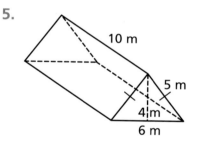

10 m

5 m

4 m

6 m

Surface area =

Show your work on your paper or in your journal.

6.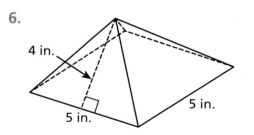

4 in.

5 in.

5 in.

Surface area =

Name the solid that can be made from the net.

7.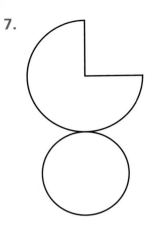

8.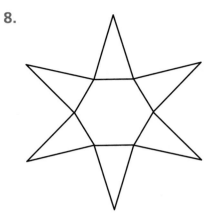

9. Name one way cylinders and cones are similar. Name one way they are different.

10. **Extended Response** Name the figure. Draw the views of the figure.

Front View	Side View	Top View

Vocabulary
negative number

▶ Negative Numbers in the Real World

A **negative number** is a number that is less than 0, for example,
⁻1, ⁻2, ⁻3, ⁻4, ⁻5, and so on.

1. List real-world situations in which negative numbers are used.

▶ Compare Positive and Negative Numbers

A number line can be extended to include negative numbers.
Such number lines include positive numbers, negative
numbers, and 0.

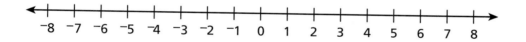

On a number line, the number farther to the right is the
greater number.

Compare the following numbers on a number line.
Write >, <, or =.

2. 5 ◯ 8   3. ⁻2 ◯ ⁻6   4. 3 ◯ ⁻3   5. ⁻1 ◯ 0

6. ⁻6 ◯ 7   7. 1 ◯ ⁻4   8. ⁻8 ◯ ⁻7   9. 0 ◯ ⁻5

Write the numbers in order from greatest to least.

10. 4, ⁻7, ⁻5, 2

11. ⁻1, 3, ⁻6, ⁻2

12. Discuss patterns you see in comparing positive and negative
    numbers, just positive numbers, and just negative numbers.

▶ Distance on a Number Line

Use the number line to find the distance between each pair of numbers.

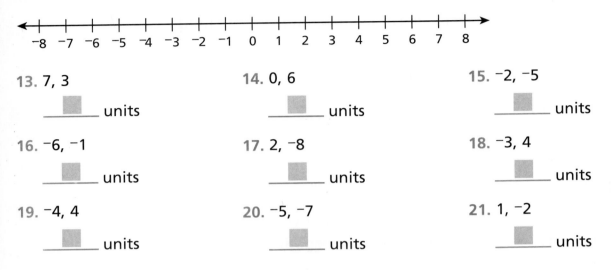

13. 7, 3

_____ units

14. 0, 6

_____ units

15. ⁻2, ⁻5

_____ units

16. ⁻6, ⁻1

_____ units

17. 2, ⁻8

_____ units

18. ⁻3, 4

_____ units

19. ⁻4, 4

_____ units

20. ⁻5, ⁻7

_____ units

21. 1, ⁻2

_____ units

Play Distance Duo with a classmate.

22.

Distance Duo			
Number Rolled	**Number Rolled**	**Distance in Units**	**Points Scored**
a.			
b.			
c.			
d.			
e.			
f.			
Total Points:			

Show your work on your paper or in your Activity Workbook.

▶ Use Models to Add Integers

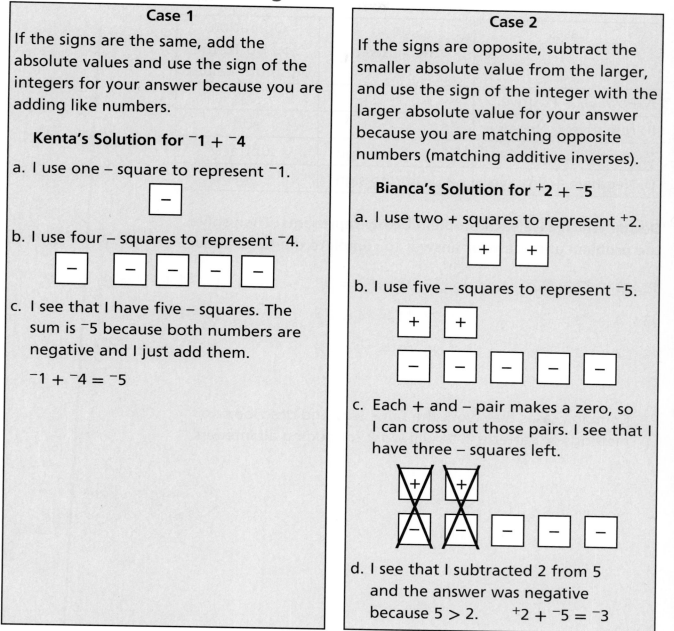

Case 1

If the signs are the same, add the absolute values and use the sign of the integers for your answer because you are adding like numbers.

Kenta's Solution for ⁻1 + ⁻4

a. I use one – square to represent ⁻1.

| – |

b. I use four – squares to represent ⁻4.

| – | | – | | – | | – | | – |

c. I see that I have five – squares. The sum is ⁻5 because both numbers are negative and I just add them.

$$^-1 + {}^-4 = {}^-5$$

Case 2

If the signs are opposite, subtract the smaller absolute value from the larger, and use the sign of the integer with the larger absolute value for your answer because you are matching opposite numbers (matching additive inverses).

Bianca's Solution for ⁺2 + ⁻5

a. I use two + squares to represent ⁺2.

| + | | + |

b. I use five – squares to represent ⁻5.

| + | | + |

| – | | – | | – | | – | | – |

c. Each + and – pair makes a zero, so I can cross out those pairs. I see that I have three – squares left.

d. I see that I subtracted 2 from 5 and the answer was negative because 5 > 2. $$^+2 + {}^-5 = {}^-3$$

Add. Use +/− squares or make a sketch if you need to.

1. ⁻3 + ⁻1 = ▨

2. ⁻3 + ⁺1 = ▨

3. ⁺2 + ⁺2 = ▨

4. ⁺2 + ⁻4 = ▨

5. ⁺10 + ⁻10 = ▨

6. ⁻10 + ⁺9 = ▨

7. ⁺15 + ⁻10 = ▨

8. ⁻30 + ⁻20 = ▨

9. ⁻6 + ⁺4 = ▨

10. ⁺4 + ⁻6 = ▨

11. ⁻30 + ⁺7 = ▨

12. ⁻100 + ⁻200 = ▨

▶ Use Absolute Values to Add Integers

Cases	Sign of the Answer	Operation You Do To the Absolute Values
A. Positive + Positive	+	
B. Negative + Negative	−	add
C. Positive + Negative	+, −, or no sign	subtract
D. Negative + Positive	+, −, or no sign	

Decide which case each problem below represents. Then solve the problem and use your answer to complete the table above.

13. $^+3 + {}^+2 =$ ▨

14. $^-3 + {}^-2 =$ ▨

15. $^+4 + {}^-3 =$ ▨

16. $^-4 + {}^+3 =$ ▨

17. $^+1 + {}^+4 =$ ▨

18. $^-1 + {}^-4 =$ ▨

19. $^+2 + {}^-2 =$ ▨

20. $^-2 + {}^+5 =$ ▨

21. $^+5 + {}^-4 =$ ▨

22. Combine cases that work the same way and describe two methods or patterns that will work for adding all integers.

Show your work on your paper or in your journal.

Show your work on your Activity Workbook page.

▶ Use Number Lines to Add Integers

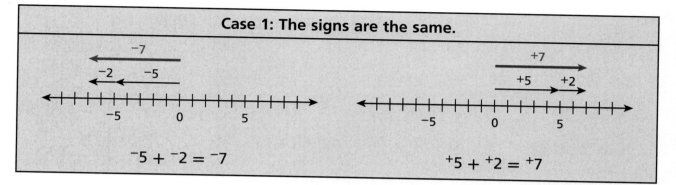

Case 1: The signs are the same.

$^-5 + {}^-2 = {}^-7$

$^+5 + {}^+2 = {}^+7$

Draw arrows to show and solve these problems.

1.

2.

$^-4 + {}^-3 = \blacksquare$

$^+4 + {}^+3 = \blacksquare$

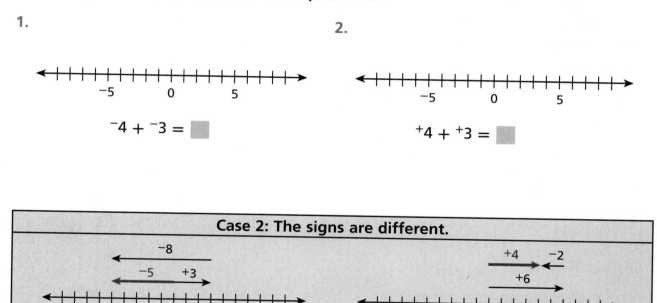

Case 2: The signs are different.

$^+3 + {}^-8 = {}^-5$

$^+6 + {}^-2 = {}^+4$

Draw arrows to show and solve these problems.

3.

4.

$^-2 + {}^+7 = \blacksquare$

$^-5 + {}^+2 = \blacksquare$

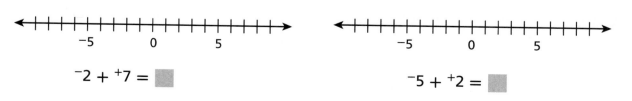

▶ Use Any Method

Add.

5. $^{+}1 + {}^{-}4 = $ ▢

6. $^{-}9 + {}^{-}2 = $ ▢

7. $^{-}2 + {}^{+}5 = $ ▢

8. $^{+}4 + {}^{+}7 = $ ▢

9. $^{-}3 + {}^{+}9 = $ ▢

10. $^{+}3 + {}^{+}5 = $ ▢

11. $^{-}8 + {}^{-}2 = $ ▢

12. $^{+}6 + {}^{-}5 = $ ▢

13. $7 + 6 = $ ▢

14. $4 + {}^{-}4 = $ ▢

15. $^{-}8 + 1 = $ ▢

16. $^{-}8 + {}^{-}8 = $ ▢

17. $^{-}10 + {}^{-}20 = $ ▢

18. $^{-}70 + 50 = $ ▢

19. $56 + {}^{-}7 = $ ▢

20. $^{-}63 + {}^{-}9 = $ ▢

On a separate sheet of paper, write the letter of the equation that best represents each situation.

21. At the beginning of the school day, the temperature was $^{-}1°C$. During the day, the temperature rose $7°C$. What was the temperature at the end of the school day?

 a. $1 + 7 = 8$

 b. $^{-}1 + 7 = 6$

 c. $1 + {}^{-}7 = {}^{-}6$

 d. $^{-}1 + {}^{-}7 = {}^{-}8$

22. A checking account had a balance of $26 before a check was written for $10. What was the balance in the checking account after the check was written?

 a. $^{-}26 + {}^{-}10 = {}^{-}36$

 b. $^{-}26 + 10 = {}^{-}16$

 c. $26 + {}^{-}10 = 16$

 d. $26 + 10 = 36$

▶ Make Generalizations

23. Write an equation that proves the statement below to be true.

 The sum of a positive integer and a negative integer is a positive integer.

24. Write an equation that proves the statement below to be true.

 The sum of a positive integer and a negative integer is a negative integer.

25. Write a generalization about the sum of a positive integer and a negative integer.

Show your work on your Activity Workbook page.

▶ Graph Positive Integers

1. The table below shows the coordinates of five points on the line $y = x + 2$. Plot the points and use your ruler to connect them with a line. Then label the line with its equation.

$y = x + 2$	
x	**y**
2	4
3	5
4	6
5	7
6	8

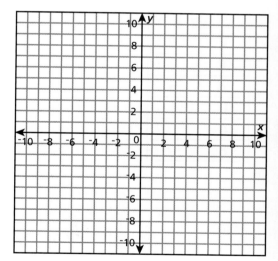

2. What pattern can you see in the signs of the x- and y-coordinates for points in the first quadrant?

▶ Graph Positive and Negative Integers

3. The table below shows the coordinates of five points on the line $y = {}^-x - 2$. Plot the points and use your ruler to connect them with a line. Then label the line with its equation.

$y = {}^-x - 2$	
x	**y**
−3	1
−2	0
−1	−1
0	−2
1	−3

4. What pattern can you see in the signs of the x- and y-coordinates for a point in the second quadrant? Third quadrant? Fourth quadrant?

> Show your work on your Activity Workbook page.

▶ Practice Graphing Integers

5. The table below shows the coordinates of five points on the line $y = x - 3$. Plot the points and use your ruler to connect them with a line. Then label the line with its equation.

$y = x - 3$	
x	y
−6	−9
−3	−6
0	−3
3	0
6	3

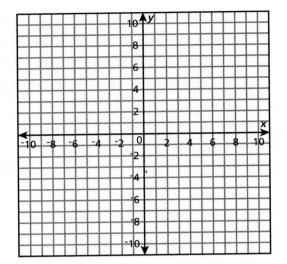

6. The table below shows the coordinates of five points on the line $y = {}^-x + 1$. Plot the points and use your ruler to connect them with a line. Then label the line with its equation.

$y = {}^-x + 1$	
x	y
−8	9
−4	5
0	1
4	−3
8	−7

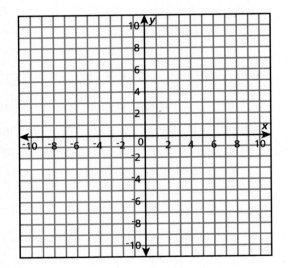

E-4
Class Activity

> Show your work on your Activity Workbook page.

▶ Write and Graph Equations

7. Complete the function table, plot the points, and use your ruler to connect the points with a line. Then label the line with its equation.

y = x + 3	
x	y
−6	
−4	
−2	
0	
2	

8. Complete the function table, plot the points, and use your ruler to connect the points with a line. Then label the line with its equation.

y = x − 1	
x	y
3	
2	
1	
0	
−1	

Show your work on your Activity Workbook page.

9. Write an equation to represent all of the values in each table. Then graph each line and label it with its equation.

x	y
−2	−1
−1	0
0	1
1	2
2	3

x	y
0	0
1	2
2	4
3	6
4	8

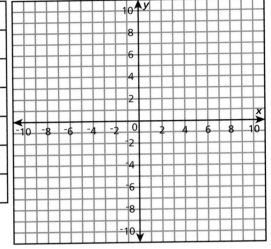

10. Write an equation to represent all of the values in each table. Then graph each line and label it with its equation.

x	y
−6	−2
−3	1
0	4
3	7
6	10

x	y
−2	−4
−1	−3
0	−2
1	−1
2	0

Show your work on your Activity Workbook page.

► Graph Real-World Situations

A taxi service charges $4 per ride, plus $2 per mile.

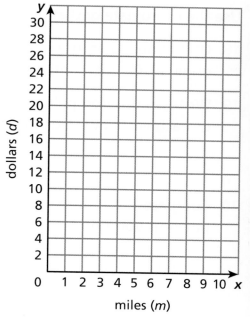

11. At the top of the table below, write an equation that describes the cost of a ride in dollars (d) for any number of miles (m).

m	d

12. Complete the table to show the cost of these rides:

   1 mile   2 miles   4 miles   5 miles   10 miles

13. On the grid at the right, graph the relationship.

14. What ordered pair represents the cost of a 7-mile ride?

15. What ordered pair represents the distance of a ride if the cost of the ride is $50?

16. Suppose the line you drew for exercise 13 was extended. Would the point (48, 100) be on the line? Explain why or why not.

17. Mia's checking account has a balance of $20 and a monthly service charge of $5. Mia never uses the account. Make a table showing the balance in the account each month for six months. Find the equation for this function and graph it.

Show your work on your Activity Workbook page.

▶ Explore Graphing Patterns

Use the coordinate grid at the right for exercises 18–20.

18. Using your ruler, draw a square that has the origin (0, 0) as its center.

19. Write an ordered pair to describe the location of each vertex of your square.

20. Compare the ordered pairs and describe the patterns you find.

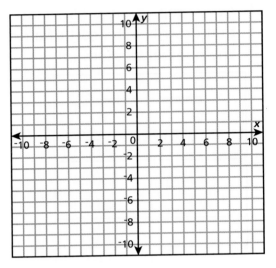

Use the coordinate grid at the right for exercises 21–23.

21. Plot a point at (⁻7, 0). Name two points on the y-axis that will form an isosceles triangle with (⁻7, 0).

22. Compare the ordered pairs and describe the patterns you find.

23. How would your patterns change if the first point was plotted on the y-axis and the next two points were plotted on the x-axis? Sketch an example to support your answer.

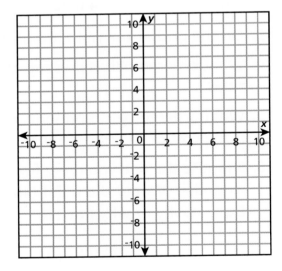

Integers and the Coordinate Plane

Glossary

acre A measure of land area. An acre is equal to 4,840 square yards.

acute angle An angle whose measure is less than 90°.

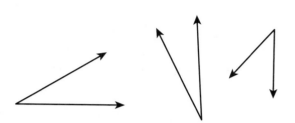

acute triangle A triangle with three acute angles.

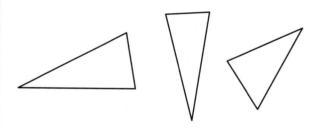

addend One of two or more numbers added together to find a sum.

Example:

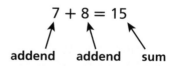

$$7 + 8 = 15$$

addend   addend   sum

Add On Method for Subtraction Find the difference between two numbers by adding to the lesser number to get the greater number.

adjusted estimate A new estimate that is made using the Digit-by-Digit method of dividing when an overestimate or underestimate has been initially made.

analog clock A clock that uses an hour hand and a minute hand to display time. Most are circular and have a face numbered from 1 to 12. Some analog clocks also have a second hand.

angle A figure formed by two rays or line segments with a common endpoint.

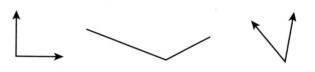

apex The vertex of a cone.

area The amount of surface covered by a figure measured in square units.

array An arrangement of objects, symbols, or numbers in equal rows and equal columns.

Associative Property of Addition Changing the grouping of addends does not change the sum.

Example:
$$3 + (5 + 7) = (3 + 5) + 7$$

Associative Property of Multiplication Changing the grouping of factors does not change the product.

Example:
$$3 \times (5 \times 7) = (3 \times 5) \times 7$$

average (See **mean**)

axis A line, usually horizontal or vertical, that is labeled with numbers or words to show the meaning of a graph.

axis of rotation A line about which a figure is rotated.

Glossary (Continued)

B

bar graph A graph that uses bars to show data.

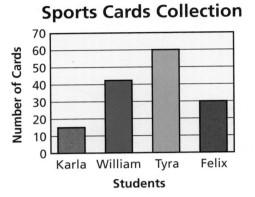

Sports Cards Collection

base of a figure For a triangle or parallelogram, a base is any side. For a trapezoid, a base is either of the parallel sides. For a prism, a base is one of the congruent parallel faces. For a pyramid, the base is the face that does not touch the vertex of the pyramid.

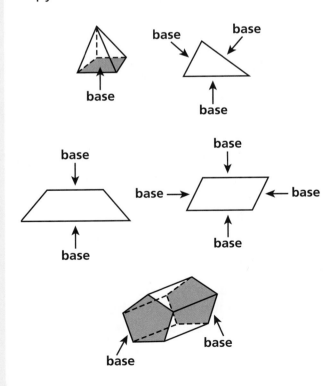

base of a power The number that is used as a factor when evaluating powers.

Example: In 10^3, the 10 is the base.

basic ratio A ratio in simplest form.

Example: The ratio 12 to 8 simplifies to 3 to 2.

billion One thousand million.
$$1,000,000,000$$

billionth One thousandth of a millionth.
$$0.000000001$$

C

capacity A measure of how much a container can hold.

categorical data Data expressed as words that represent categories.

Example: Color (red, blue, yellow, and so on)

Celsius The metric temperature scale. Water freezes at 0°C and boils at 100°C.

centimeter A unit of measure in the metric system that equals one hundredth of a meter. 1 cm = 0.01 m

1 cm

change minus A change situation that can be represented by subtraction. In a change minus situation, the starting number, the change, or the result will be unknown.

Example:

Unknown Start	Unknown Change	Unknown Result
$n - 2 = 3$	$5 - n = 3$	$5 - 2 = n$

change plus A change situation that can be represented by addition. In a change plus situation, the starting number, the change, or the result will be unknown.

Example:

Unknown Start	Unknown Change	Unknown Result
$n + 2 = 5$	$3 + n = 5$	$3 + 2 = n$

circle A plane figure that forms a closed path so that all the points on the path are the same distance from a point called the center.

circle graph A graph that uses parts of a circle to show data.

Zak's Book Collection

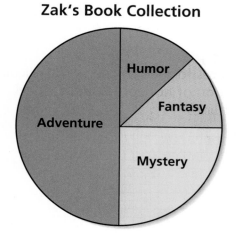

circumference The distance around a circle.

clockwise The direction in which the hands of a clock move.

collection situations Situations that involve putting together (joining) or taking apart (separating) groups.

column A part of a table or array that contains items arranged vertically.

combination situation A combination situation is one in which pairs or sets are counted. Tables can be used to show combinations.

Types of Sandwiches		
	Cheese	**Peanut Butter**	**Tuna**
White	W + C	W + PB	W + T
Wheat	Wh + C	Wh + PB	Wh + T

common denominator A common multiple of two or more denominators.

Example: 6 could be used as a common denominator for $\frac{1}{2}$ and $\frac{1}{3}$.

$$\frac{1}{2} = \frac{3}{6} \qquad \frac{1}{3} = \frac{2}{6}$$

so $\frac{1}{2} + \frac{1}{3} = \frac{3}{6} + \frac{2}{6} = \frac{5}{6}$

Commutative Property of Addition Changing the order of addends does not change the sum.

Example: $3 + 8 = 8 + 3$

Commutative Property of Multiplication Changing the order of factors does not change the product.

Example: $3 \times 8 = 8 \times 3$

comparison situation A situation in which two amounts are compared by addition or by multiplication. An additive comparison situation compares by asking or telling how much more (how much less) one amount is than

Glossary (Continued)

another. A multiplicative comparison situation compares by asking or telling how many times as many one amount is as another. The multiplicative comparison may also be made using fraction language. For example, you can say, "Sally has one fourth as much as Tom has," instead of saying "Tom has 4 times as much as Sally has."

complementary angles Two angles having a sum of 90°.

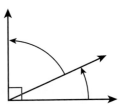

complex figure A figure made by combining simple geometric figures like rectangles and triangles.

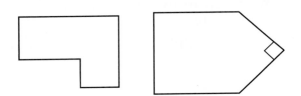

composite number A number greater than 1 that has more than one factor pair. Examples of composite numbers are 4, 15, and 45. The factor pairs of 15 are: 1 and 15, 3 and 5.

cone A solid figure with a curved base and a single vertex.

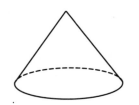

congruent Exactly the same size and shape.

Example: Triangles *ABC* and *PQR* are congruent.

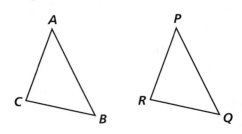

continuous data Data that represent an accumulation without interruption. Each data point is related to the data point before and after it.

Example: Temperature reading over a 24-hour period: 45°, 47°, 52° and so on.

coordinate A number that determines the position of a point in one direction on a grid.

coordinate plane A system of coordinates formed by the perpendicular intersection of horizontal and vertical number lines.

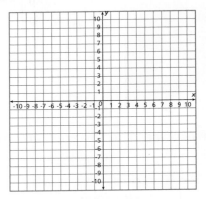

counterclockwise The direction opposite to the direction the hands of a clock move.

counterexample An example that proves that a general statement is false.

cube A rectangular prism that has 6 faces that are congruent squares.

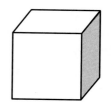

cubic centimeter A metric unit for measuring volume. It is the volume of a cube with one-centimeter edges.

cubic meter A metric unit for measuring volume. It is the volume of a cube with one-meter edges.

cubic unit A unit of volume made by a cube with all edges one unit long.

Example: Cubic centimeters and cubic inches are cubic units.

cup A U.S. customary unit of capacity equal to half a pint.

cylinder A solid (three-dimensional) figure with two curved, congruent bases.

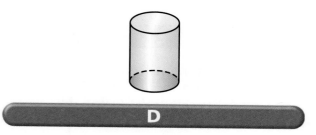

D

data Pieces of information.

decimal number A representation of a number using the numerals 0 to 9, in which each digit has a value 10 times the digit to its right. A dot or decimal point separates the whole-number part of the number on the left from the fractional part on the right.

decimeter A unit of measure in the metric system that equals one tenth of a meter. 1 dm = 0.1 m

degree A unit for measuring angles. Also a unit for measuring temperature. (See Celsius and Fahrenheit.)

denominator The number below the bar in a fraction. It tells the number of unit fractions into which the 1 whole is divided.

Example: 4 is the denominator.

$$\frac{3}{4} \longleftarrow \text{denominator}$$

diagonal A line segment connecting two vertices that are not next to each other.

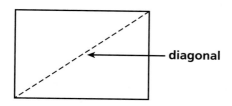

diameter A line segment from one side of a circle to the other through the center. Also the length of that segment.

difference The result of a subtraction.
Example: $54 - 37 = 17$
↑— difference

digit Any of the symbols 0, 1, 2, 3, 4, 5, 6, 7, 8, or 9.

Glossary (Continued)

digital clock A clock that has a colon (:) separating digits representing hours from digits representing minutes. Some digital clocks also have another colon to separate minutes from seconds. Digital clocks also display A.M. or P.M.

Digit-by-Digit A method used to solve a division problem.

Example:

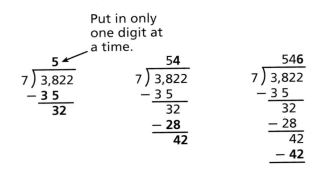

Put in only one digit at a time.

dimension The height, length, or width.

Examples:

A line segment has only length, so it has *one* dimension.

A rectangle has length and width, so it has *two* dimensions.

A cube has length, width, and height, so it has *three* dimensions.

discrete data Data that involve counting. In a set of discrete data, each number is exact and the numbers are not related to each other.

Example: The heights of five trees: 18 ft, 35 ft, 20 ft, 40 ft, 28 ft.

Distributive Property You can multiply a sum by a number, or multiply each addend by the number and add the products; the result is the same.

Example:
$$3 \times (2 + 4) = (3 \times 2) + (3 \times 4)$$
$$3 \times 6 \ = \ 6 \ + \ 12$$
$$18 \ = \ 18$$

divisible A number is divisible by another number if the quotient is a whole number with no remainder.

Example: 15 is divisible by 5 because $15 \div 5 = 3$

dot array An arrangement of dots in rows and columns.

double bar graph Data is compared by using pairs of bars drawn next to each other.

Number of Rainy Days in Florida and Texas

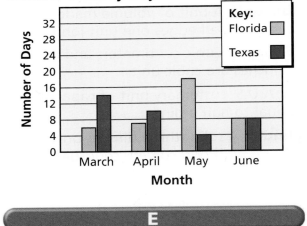

E

edge A line segment that forms as a side of a two-dimensional figure or the part of a three-dimensional figure where two faces meet.

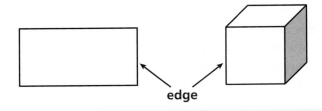

edge

elapsed time The amount of time that passes between two times.

equal groups Groups that have the same number of objects.

equation A statement that two expressions are equal. An equation always has an equals sign.

Example: $32 + 35 = 67$
$50 = 75 - 25$
$1 + 10 + 40 = 53 - 2$

equilateral Having all equal sides.

Example: An equilateral triangle

equivalent Representing the same number or amount.

equivalent fractions Two or more fractions that represent the same fractional part of 1 whole.

estimate Find *about* how many or *about* how much. A reasonable guess about a measurement or answer.

evaluate To substitute a value for a letter and then calculate to simplify the expression.

even number A whole number that is a multiple of 2. An even number ends with a 0, 2, 4, 6, or 8.

Example: 68 is an even number because it is a multiple of 2; $2 \times 34 = 68$.

example A specific instance that demonstrates a general statement.

expanded form A way of writing a number that shows the value of each of its digits.

Example: Expanded form of 835:
$800 + 30 + 5$
8 hundreds + 3 tens + 5 ones

Expanded Notation A strategy used to solve multiplication and division problems.

$$67 \times 43$$

$43 = 40 + 3$
$\times\ 67 = 60 + 7$

$60 \times 40 = 2,400$
$60 \times\ \ 3 = \ \ \ 180$
$7 \times 40 = \ \ \ 280$
$7 \times\ \ 3 = \ \ \ \ \ 21$
$\underline{}\ 2,881$

$\begin{array}{r} 43 \\ \times\ 67 \\ \hline 2,400 \\ 180 \\ 280 \\ 21 \\ \hline 2,881 \end{array}$

$$3,822 \div 7$$

Show the zeros in the places.

$\begin{array}{r} 500 \\ 7\overline{)3,822} \\ -\ 3,500 \\ \hline 322 \end{array}$

$\begin{array}{r} 40 \\ 500 \\ 7\overline{)3,822} \\ -\ 3,500 \\ \hline 322 \\ -\ 280 \\ \hline 42 \end{array}$

$\begin{array}{r} 6 \\ 40 \\ 500 \\ 7\overline{)3,822} \\ -\ 3,500 \\ \hline 322 \\ -\ 280 \\ \hline 42 \\ -\ 42 \end{array}$ $40\overline{)546}$

expression A combination of one or more numbers, variables, or numbers and variables with one or more operations.

Examples: 4
$6n$
$6n - 5$
$7 + 4$
$2(3 + 4)$

exponent The number in a power that tells how many times the base is used as a factor.

Example: In 10^3, the 3 is the exponent.

F

face A flat surface of a three-dimensional figure.

Glossary (Continued)

factor One of two or more numbers multiplied together to make a product.

Example:

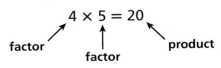

$$4 \times 5 = 20$$

factor   factor   product

Factor Puzzle A two-by-two table that is made from the cells in two rows and two columns of the Multiplication Table. It can be used to solve proportions. The unknown number in the ◯ will be $5 \times 3 = 15$.

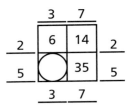

Fahrenheit The temperature scale used in the United States. Water freezes at 32°F and boils at 212°F.

floor plan A scale drawing of a room as seen from above.

foot A U.S. customary unit of length equal to 12 inches and $\frac{1}{3}$ yard.

fraction A number that is the sum of unit fractions, each an equal part of a set or part of a whole.

Examples: $\frac{3}{4} = \frac{1}{4} + \frac{1}{4} + \frac{1}{4}$

$\frac{5}{4} = \frac{1}{4} + \frac{1}{4} + \frac{1}{4} + \frac{1}{4} + \frac{1}{4}$

front-end estimation A method of estimating that uses the left-most digit in each number and replaces all of the other digits with zeros.

Example:

$$4,588 \longrightarrow 4,000$$
$$-2,616 \longrightarrow -2,000$$
$$2,000 \text{ estimated difference}$$

function A consistent relationship between two sets of numbers. Each number in one of the sets is paired with exactly one number in the other set. A function can be shown in a chart, or as a set of ordered pairs.

Example: The relationship between the number of yards and the number of feet.

$$f = 3y$$

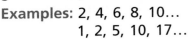

Yards	1	2	3	4	5	6	7
Feet	3	6	9	12	15	18	21

G

gallon A U.S. customary unit of capacity equal to 4 quarts, 8 pints, and 16 cups.

gram The basic unit of mass in the metric system.

greater than (>) A symbol used when comparing two numbers. The greater number is given first.

Example: 33 > 17
33 is greater than 17.

greatest Largest.

growing pattern A number or geometric pattern that increases.

Examples: 2, 4, 6, 8, 10…
1, 2, 5, 10, 17…

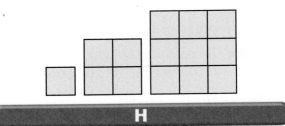

H

half turn A 180° rotation.

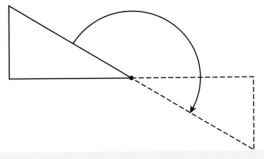

height The perpendicular distance from a base of a figure to the highest point.

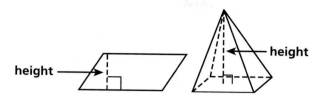

hexagon A six-sided polygon.

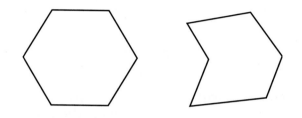

histogram A graph in which bars are used to display how frequently data occurs between intervals.

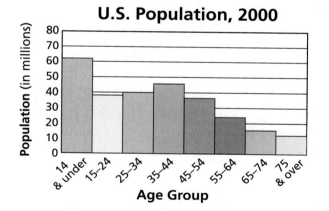

hypothesis A statement used as the basis of an investigation.

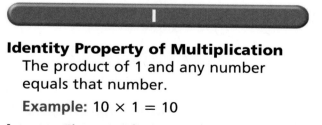

Identity Property of Multiplication The product of 1 and any number equals that number.

Example: $10 \times 1 = 10$

image The new figure that results from the translation, reflection, or rotation of a figure.

improper fraction A fraction whose numerator is greater than or equal to the denominator.

Example: $\frac{3}{2}$

inch A U.S. customary unit of length. There are 12 inches in 1 foot.

1 inch

inequality A statement that two expressions are not equal.

Examples: $2 < 5$
$4 + 5 > 12 - 8$

integer The set of integers includes the set of positive whole numbers (1, 2, 3, …) and their opposites (–1, –2, –3, …) and 0.

inverse operations Opposite or reverse operations that undo each other. Addition and subtraction are inverse operations. Multiplication and division are inverse operations.

Examples: $4 + 6 = 10$, so $10 - 6 = 4$
$3 \times 9 = 27$, so $27 \div 9 = 3$

isosceles trapezoid A trapezoid with one pair of opposite congruent sides.

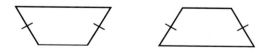

isosceles triangle A triangle with at least two congruent sides.

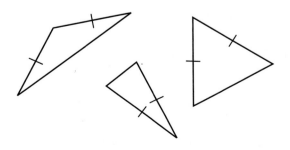

Glossary (Continued)

K

key A part of a map, graph, or chart that explains what symbols mean.

kilogram A unit of mass in the metric system that equals one thousand grams. 1 kg = 1,000 g

kiloliter A unit of capacity in the metric system that equals one thousand liters. 1 kL = 1,000 L

kilometer A unit of length in the metric system that equals one thousand meters. 1 km = 1,000 m

L

least Smallest.

least common denominator The least common multiple of two denominators. **Example:** 6 is the least common denominator of $\frac{1}{2}$ and $\frac{1}{3}$.

length The measure of a line segment, or of one side or edge of a figure.

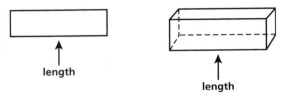

less than (<) A symbol used when comparing two numbers. The smaller number is given first.

Example: 54 < 78
54 is less than 78.

line A straight path that goes on forever in opposite directions.

Example: line *AB*

line graph A graph that uses a broken line to show changes in data.

Deer Population in Midland Park

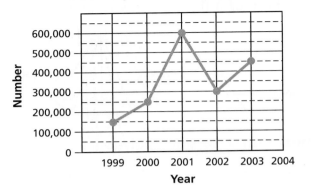

line plot A diagram that shows the frequency of data on a number line.

line of symmetry A line such that if a figure is folded on that line, the two parts will match exactly.

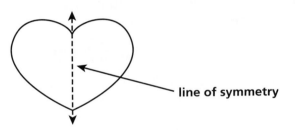

line of symmetry

line segment Part of a line that has two endpoints.

line symmetry A figure has line symmetry if it can be folded along a line to create two halves that match exactly.

Linked Multiplication Column Table A Multiplication Column Table that also has a column showing the unit that links the terms in each ratio.

Example: This table shows the ratios of two rates, $3 per day and $5 per day, and the linking unit, days.

Days	Noreen (3)	Tim (5)
0	0	0
1	3	5
2	6	10
3	9	15
4	12	20

liter The basic unit of capacity in the metric system.

M

mass The measure of the amount of matter in an object.

mean (average) The size of each of n equal groups made from n data values. The mean can be found by adding the values in a set of data and dividing by the number of such values.

Example: 75, 84, 89, 91, 101
$75 + 84 + 89 + 91 + 101 = 440$, then $440 \div 5 = 88$. The mean is 88.

measure of central tendency The mean, median, or mode of a set of numbers.

median The middle number in a set of ordered numbers. For an even number of numbers, the median is the number halfway between the two middle numbers.

Examples: 13   26   34   47   52
The median for this set is 34.
8   8   12   14   20   21
The median for this set is 13.

meter The basic unit of length in the metric system.

milligram A unit of mass in the metric system that equals one thousandth of a gram. 1 mg = 0.001 g

milliliter A unit of capacity in the metric system that equals one thousandth of a liter. 1 mL = 0.001 L

millimeter A unit of length in the metric system that equals one thousandth of a meter. 1 mm = 0.001 m

misleading A comparing sentence containing language that may trick you into doing the wrong operation.

Example: John's age is 3 *more* than Jessica's. If John is 12, how old is Jessica?

mixed number A number represented by a whole number and a fraction.

Example: $4\frac{2}{3}$

mode The number that appears most frequently in a set of numbers.

Example: 2, 4, 4, 4, 5, 7, 7
4 is the mode in this set of numbers.

Multiplication Column Table A table made of two columns from a multiplication table.

Days	Dollars
0	0
1	3
2	6
3	9
4	12
5	15
6	18
7	21
8	24
9	27

multiplication table A table that shows the product of each pair of numbers in the left column and top row.

multiplier The factor used to multiply the numerator and denominator to create an equivalent fraction.

Example: A multiplier of 5 changes $\frac{2}{3}$ to $\frac{5 \times 2}{5 \times 3} = \frac{10}{15}$.

Glossary (Continued)

N

negative number A number less than zero.

    Examples: −1, −23, and −3.5 are negative numbers.

net A flat pattern that can be folded to make a solid figure.

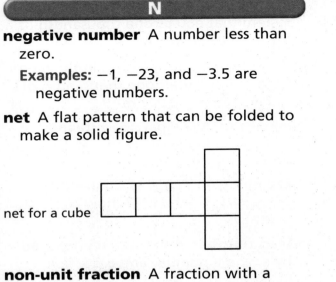

net for a cube

non-unit fraction A fraction with a numerator greater than 1.

    Examples: $\frac{3}{4}$ or $\frac{4}{8}$ or $\frac{10}{8}$.

number sentence Describes how numbers or expressions are related to each other using one of the symbols =, <, or >. The types of number sentences are equations and inequalities.

    Examples: 25 + 25 = 50
                 13 > 8 + 2

numerical data Data that consist of numbers.

numerator The number above the bar in a fraction.

    Example: The numerator is 2.

$\frac{2}{3}$ ←—— numerator

It tells how many unit fractions there are: 2 of the $\frac{1}{3}$.

O

oblique lines Lines that are not parallel or perpendicular.

obtuse angle An angle greater than a right angle and less than a straight angle.

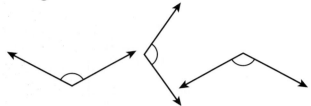

obtuse triangle A triangle with one obtuse angle.

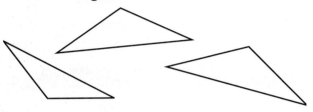

odd number A whole number that is not a multiple of 2. An odd number ends with 1, 3, 5, 7, or 9.

    Example: 73 is an odd number because it is not a multiple of 2.

one-dimensional Having only length as a measure. A line segment is one-dimensional.

operation A mathematical process. Addition, subtraction, multiplication, division, and raising a number to a power are operations.

Order of Operations A set of rules that states the order in which operations should be done.
1. Compute inside parentheses first.
2. Simplify any exponents.
3. Multiply and divide from left to right.
4. Add and subtract from left to right.

ordered pair A pair of numbers that shows the position of a point on a coordinate grid.

    Example: The ordered pair (3, 4) represents a point 3 units to the right of the *y*-axis and 4 units above the *x*-axis.

origin The point (0, 0) on a two-dimensional coordinate grid.

ounce A unit of weight or capacity in the U.S. customary system equal to one sixteenth of a pound or one eighth of a cup.

outlier A number or numbers whose values are much less or much greater than the other numbers in a data set.

overestimate An estimate that is greater than the actual amount.

Example: A shirt costs $26.47 and a pair of jeans cost $37.50. You can make an overestimate by rounding $26.47 to $30 and $37.50 to $40 to be sure you have enough money to pay for the clothes.

P

parallel The same distance apart at every point.

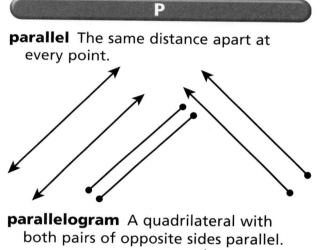

parallelogram A quadrilateral with both pairs of opposite sides parallel.

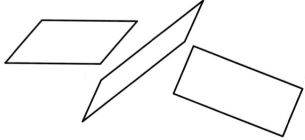

parentheses Symbols used to group numbers together.

$$7 + (3 \times 4) = 19$$

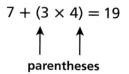

parentheses

partial products Products of the smaller problems in the Rectangle Sections method of multiplying.

Example: The partial products are highlighted.

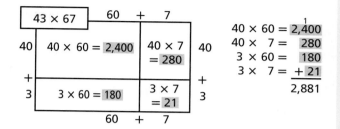

pentagon A polygon with five sides.

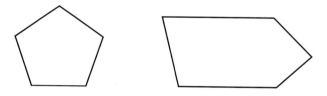

percent Percent means out of a hundred or per hundred. The numerator of a fraction that has 100 as the denominator is followed by the % sign: 50% is $\frac{50}{100}$ or a value equivalent to $\frac{50}{100}$.

perimeter The distance around a figure.

perpendicular Lines, line segments, or rays are perpendicular if they form right angles.

Example: These two lines are perpendicular.

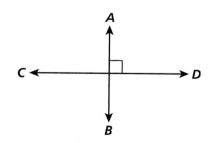

pi A number equal to the circumference of a circle divided by its diameter, or about 3.14. Pi is often represented by the symbol π.

Glossary (Continued)

pint A U.S. customary unit of capacity equal to half a quart.

place value The value assigned to the place that a digit occupies in a number.

Example: 235

The 2 is in the hundreds place, so its value is 200.

plane A flat surface that extends without end.

polygon A closed plane figure with sides made of straight line segments.

pound A unit of weight in the U.S. customary system.

pre-image A figure before its transformation.

prime factorization A whole number written as the product of prime factors.

Example: Prime factorization of 30: $2 \times 3 \times 5$

prime number A number greater than 1 that has 1 and itself as the only factor pair. Examples of prime numbers are 2, 7, and 13. The only factor pair of 7 is 1 and 7.

prism A solid figure with two congruent parallel bases.

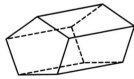

pentagonal prism

probability A number between 0 and 1 that represents the chance of an event happening.

product The result of a multiplication.

Example: $9 \times 7 = 63$

product

proof A demonstration of the truth of a general statement.

proportion An equation that shows two equivalent ratios.

Example: $6 : 10 = 9 : 15$

pyramid A solid with a polygon for a base whose vertices are all joined to a single point.

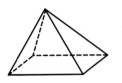

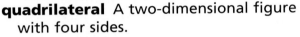
Q

quadrilateral A two-dimensional figure with four sides.

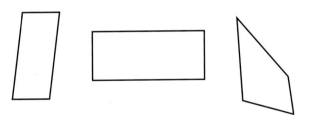

quart A U.S. customary unit of capacity equal to $\frac{1}{4}$ gallon or 2 pints.

quarter turn A 90° rotation.

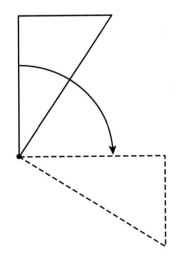

R

radius A line segment that connects the center of a circle to any point on that circle. Also the length of that line segment.

range The difference between the greatest and the least number in a set.

ratio A comparison of two or more quantities in the same units.

Ratio Table A table that shows equivalent ratios.

Example: This table show ratios equivalent to the basic ratio, 3 : 5.

③	⑤
0	0
3	5
6	10
9	15
12	20
15	25
18	30
21	35
24	40

ray A part of a line that has one endpoint and extends without end in one direction.

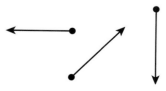

rectangle A parallelogram with four right angles.

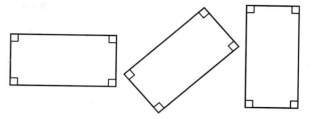

Rectangle Rows A method used to solve multiplication problems.

Example:

$$43 \times 67$$

```
        67
         2
        67
40    × 40      2,680
      2,680   + 201
  +            2,881
         2
        67
 3     ×  3
        201
```

Rectangle Sections A method used to solve multiplication and division problems.

Example:

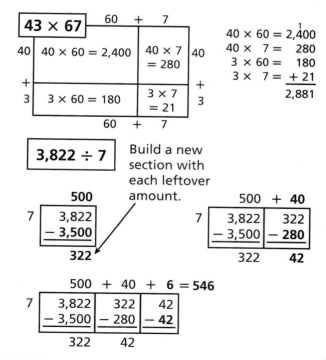

Glossary (Continued)

rectangular prism A solid that has congruent rectangular bases.

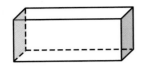

reflection A transformation that flips a figure onto a congruent image. Sometimes called a *flip*.

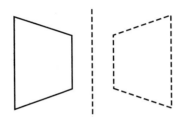

reflex angle An angle greater than 180°.

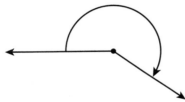

remainder The number left over after dividing a number by a number that does not divide it evenly.

Example: 43 ÷ 5 = 8 R3

The remainder is 3.

Repeated Groups Groups with the same number of objects are Repeated Groups.

Example: 2 + 2 + 2 = 6
There are 3 repeated groups of 2.

repeating pattern A pattern consisting of a group of numbers, letters, or figures that repeat.

Example: 1, 2, 1, 2, …
A, B, C, A, B, C, …

rhombus A parallelogram with congruent sides.

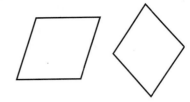

right angle An angle that measures 90°.

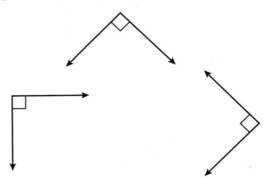

right trapezoid A trapezoid with at least one right angle.

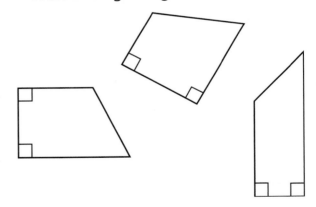

right triangle A triangle with one right angle.

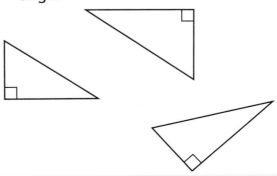

rotation A turn. A transformation that turns a figure so that each point stays an equal distance from a single point, the center of rotation.

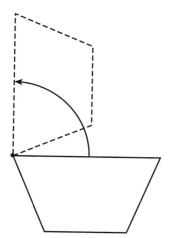

rotational symmetry The property of a figure that allows it to fit exactly on itself in less than one full rotation.

round To find the nearest ten, hundred, thousand, or some other place value.

Example: 463 rounded to the nearest ten is 460.
463 rounded to the nearest hundred is 500.

row A part of a table or array that contains items arranged horizontally.

● ● ● ● ●

S

scale Numbers or marks arranged at regular intervals that are used for measurement or to establish position. In a scale drawing, the scale tells how the measurements in the drawing relate to the actual measurements.

scale drawing A drawing that is made in proportion to the size of a real object.

scalene triangle A triangle with no equal sides is a scalene triangle.

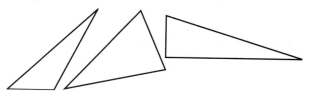

Short Cut Method A method used to solve multiplication problems.

Example: 43 × 67

Step 1	Step 2	Step 3	Step 4	Step 5
$\overset{2}{4}3$	$\overset{2}{4}3$	$\overset{2}{4}3$	$\overset{1}{\underset{2}{4}}3$	$\overset{1}{\underset{2}{4}}3$
× 67	× 67	× 67	× 67	× 67
1	301	301	301	301
		0	2,580	2,580
				2,881

short word form A way of writing a number that uses digits and words.

Example: Short word form of 12,835: 12 thousand, 835

shrinking pattern A number or geometric pattern that decreases.

Example: 15, 12, 9, 6, 3,…
25, 20, 16, 13, 11,…

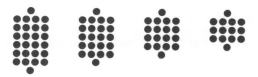

similar Having the same shape but not necessarily the same size. The lengths of the corresponding sides are in proprotion.

similar figures

Glossary (Continued)

simplest form A fraction is in simplest form if there is no whole number (other than 1) that divides evenly into the numerator and demominator.

Example: $\frac{3}{4}$ This fraction is in simplest form because no number divides evenly into 3 and 4.

simplify To find a result. To rewrite a fraction as an equivalent fraction with a smaller numerator and denominator.

Example: $\frac{3}{6} = \frac{1}{2}$

situation equation An equation that shows the action or the relationship in a problem.

Example: $35 + n = 40$

slant height The height of a triangular face of a pyramid.

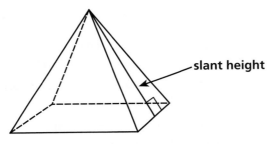

solution equation An equation that shows the operation to perform in order to solve the problem.

Example: $n = 40 - 35$

square A rectangle with four congruent sides.

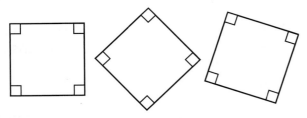

square number The product of a whole number and itself.

Example: $3 \times 3 = 9$
9 is a square number.

square root The square root of a number n is a number that when multiplied by itself equals the number n.

Examples: 4 is the square root of the number 16.

square unit A unit of area equal to the area of a square with one-unit sides.

Examples: square meters and square inches

square yard A unit of area equal to the area of a square with one-yard sides.

standard form The form of a number written using digits.

Example: 2,145

stem-and-leaf plot A display that uses place value to organize a set of data.

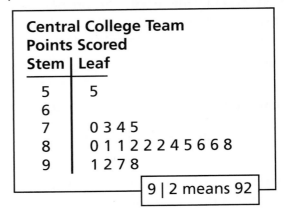

straight angle An angle of 180°.

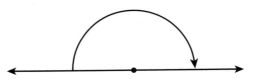

sum The result of an addition.

Example:

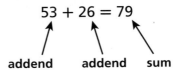

supplementary angles Two angles having a sum of 180°.

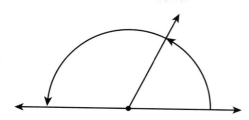

surface area The total area of the two-dimensional surfaces around the outside of a three-dimensional figure.

T

table Data arranged in rows and columns.

term in a pattern A number, letter, or figure in a pattern.

Example: The second term in this number pattern is 10.

5, 10, 15, 20, 25,…

three-dimensional Having length measurements in three directions, perpendicular to each other.

ton A unit of weight or mass that equals 2,000 pounds.

tonne A metric unit of mass that equals 1,000 kilograms.

transformation Reflections, rotations, and translations are examples of tranformations.

translation A transformation that moves a figure along a straight line without turning or flipping. Sometimes called a *slide*.

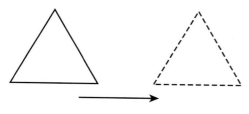

trapezoid A quadrilateral with exactly one pair of parallel sides.

triangle A polygon with three sides.

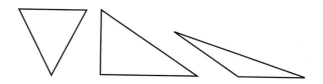

two-dimensional Having length measurements in two directions that are perpendicular to each other.

U

underestimate An estimate that is less than the actual amount.

Example: A shirt costs $26.47 and a pair of jeans cost $37.50. If you brought $60 to pay for the clothes because you rounded $26.47 to $25 and $37.50 to $35, you made an under-estimate and did not have enough money.

ungroup Rewrite a mixed number with a different whole number and fraction part or rewrite a whole number with different numbers in the places.

Example: $4\frac{2}{3} = 3\frac{5}{3}$ or $100 + 20 + 3 = 90 + 30 + 3$

unit Something used repeatedly to measure quantity.

Examples: Centimeters, pounds, inches, and so on.

unit fraction A fraction with a numerator of 1.

Examples: $\frac{1}{2}$ and $\frac{1}{10}$

Glossary (Continued)

unsimplify Rewrite a fraction as an equivalent fraction with a greater numerator and denominator.

Examples: $\frac{1}{2} = \frac{3}{6}$

V

variable A letter or symbol that represents a number.

Venn Diagram A diagram that uses overlapping circles to show the relationship between two (or more) sets of objects.

Example: This Venn diagram shows that of 25 students surveyed, 12 like the color blue, 10 like the color orange, and 3 like both colors.

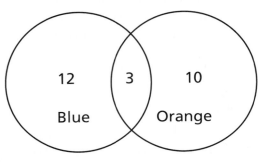

vertex A point that is shared by two arms of an angle, two sides of a polygon, or edges of a solid figure. The point of a cone.

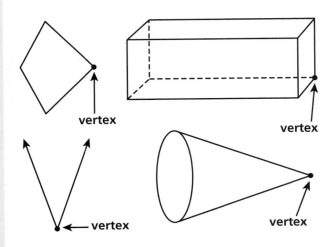

view A two-dimensional representation of what a three-dimensional figure looks like from the front, side, or top.

volume The measure of the amount of space occupied by an object.

W

width The measure of one side or edge of a figure.

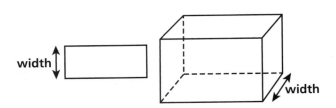

word form The form of a number written using words instead of digits.

Example: Six hundred thirty-nine

X

x-axis The horizontal axis of a two-dimensional coordinate grid.

x-coordinate A number that represents a point's horizontal distance from the y-axis of a two-dimensional coordinate grid.

Y

y-axis The vertical axis of a two-dimensional coordinate grid.

yard A U.S. customary unit of length equal to 3 feet or 36 inches.

y-coordinate A number that represents a point's vertical distance from the x-axis of a two-dimensional coordinate grid.

Multiplication Table and Scrambled Tables (Volume 2)

E

×	4	2	5	1	3	8	10	7	9	6
4	16	8	20	4	12	32	40	28	36	24
1	4	2	5	1	3	8	10	7	9	6
2	8	4	10	2	6	16	20	14	18	12
5	20	10	25	5	15	40	50	35	45	30
3	12	6	15	3	9	24	30	21	27	18
9	36	18	45	9	27	72	90	63	81	54
6	24	12	30	6	18	48	60	42	54	36
10	40	20	50	10	30	80	100	70	90	60
7	28	14	35	7	21	56	70	49	63	42
8	32	16	40	8	24	64	80	56	72	48

F

×	9	8	6	7	4	6	8	7	4	9
2	18	16	12	14	8	12	16	14	8	18
3	27	24	18	21	12	18	24	21	12	27
5	45	40	30	35	20	30	40	35	20	45
3	27	24	18	21	12	18	24	21	12	27
5	45	40	30	35	20	30	40	35	20	45
9	81	72	54	63	36	54	72	63	36	81
7	63	56	42	49	28	42	56	49	28	63
6	54	48	36	42	24	36	48	42	24	54
8	72	64	48	56	32	48	64	56	32	72
4	36	32	24	28	16	24	32	28	16	36

G

×	7	6	8	7	8	6	8	7	6	8
5	35	30	40	35	40	30	40	35	30	40
4	28	24	32	28	32	24	32	28	24	32
3	21	18	24	21	24	18	24	21	18	24
2	14	12	16	14	16	12	16	14	12	16
8	56	48	64	56	64	48	64	56	48	64
9	63	54	72	63	72	54	72	63	54	72
7	49	42	56	49	56	42	56	49	42	56
6	42	36	48	42	48	36	48	42	36	48
8	56	48	64	56	64	48	64	56	48	64
6	42	36	48	42	48	36	48	42	36	48

H

×	4	6	7	8	9	6	9	8	7	4
4	16	24	28	32	36	24	36	32	28	16
6	24	36	42	48	54	36	54	48	42	24
7	28	42	49	56	63	42	63	56	49	28
8	32	48	56	64	72	48	72	64	56	32
9	36	54	63	72	81	54	81	72	63	36
8	32	48	56	64	72	48	72	64	56	32
9	36	54	63	72	81	54	81	72	63	36
4	16	24	28	32	36	24	36	32	28	16
7	28	42	49	56	63	42	63	56	49	28
6	24	36	42	48	54	36	54	48	42	24